BEYOND THE VEIL

BEYOND THE VEIL

Male-Female Dynamics
in a Modern Muslim Society

by

FATIMA MERNISSI

SCHENKMAN PUBLISHING COMPANY

Halsted Press Division
John Wiley and Sons
New York   London   Sydney   Toronto

Copyright © 1975
SCHENKMAN PUBLISHING COMPANY, Inc.
Cambridge, Massachusetts 02138

Distributed solely by Halsted Press, a Division
of John Wiley & Sons, Inc., New York

Library of Congress Cataloging in Publication Data
Main entry under title:

Mernissi, Fatima.
Beyond The Veil.

Bibliography: p.
1. Women, Muslim. I. Title.
HQ1170.M46   301.41'2'0917671   75-29283

CLOTH — 0 470-59612-0
PAPER — 0 470-59613-9

CONTENTS

v

For The Western Reader

Is there a nascent female liberation movement similar to those appearing in Western countries? This kind of question has for decades blocked and distorted analysis of the Muslim woman's situation, keeping it at the level of senseless comparisons and unfounded conclusions. It is a well-established tradition to discuss the Muslim woman by comparing her, implictly or explicitly, to the Western woman. This tradition reflects the general pattern prevailing in both East and West when the issue is "who is more civilized than whom."

When the Muslim countries were defeated and occupied by the West, the colonizers used all available means to persuade the defeated Muslims of their inferiority in order to justify foreign occupation. Muslims were dismissed as promiscuous, and many crocodile tears were shed over the terrible fate of the Muslim woman. In this situation Muslims found themselves defending anachronistic institutions (by many Muslim's own standards) such as polygamy, arguing for example that it is better to institutionalize man's polygamous desires than to force him to have secret mistresses.

Unfortunately the argument was not between the colonizers and ordinary Muslims, but between the colonizers and representatives of the nationalist movement, the intellectuals who had previously supported the liberation of Muslim women. Two legacies of this conflict are still influencing the situation of women in the Muslim world:

1. The fact that Western colonizers took over the paternalistic defense of the Muslim woman's lot characterized any changes in her condition as concessions to the colonizer. Since the external aspects of women's liberation, for example the neglect of the veil for western dress, were often emulations of Western women, women's liberation was readily identified as succumbing to foreign influences.

2. The women's liberation problem has been viewed almost exclusively as a religious problem. The nationalist movement started as a religious movement, and the fight against the West was perceived and lived very much as a modern religious crusade. The nationalists had advocated the liberation of women, in the name of Islam's triumph, not in the name of any genuine modern global ideology. The eclectic variety of meanings given by kings and Palestinians and Maoists to "Muslim socialism" demonstrates that such an ideology is still lacking.

In this book, I am not concerned with contrasting the way women are treated in Muslim East with the way they are treated in the Christian West. I believe sexual inequality is the basis of both systems. My aim is not to clarify which situation is better, but to understand the sexual dynamics of the Muslim world. I use comparisons between East and West only when they underline the *sui-generis* pattern of the heterosexual relationship in the Muslim system.

I am also not concerned with analyzing women as an entity separate from men; rather, I try to explore the male-female relation as an entity within the Muslim system, a basic element of its structure. It appears to me that the Muslim system is not so much opposed to women as to the heterosexual unit. What is feared is the growth of the involvement between a man and a woman into an all-encompassing love, satisfying the sexual, emotional and intellectual needs of both partners. Such an involvement constitutes a direct threat to the man's allegiance to Allah, which should be the unconditional investment of all the man's energies, thoughts and feelings in his God.

The change in the sexes' relations has been one of the most explosive threats that Muslim society has had to face in the twentieth century, and its dilemma has been expounded in a prolific literature concerning the relation between Islam and the woman.[1] Muslim societies, defeated, occupied and dominated by foreign infidel powers, have come to the conclusion that the only way to alleviate foreign domination is to free the whole Muslim "person-power" by involving both men and women in the production process. But to achieve that aim, Muslim society would have to grant the women, now needed as workers or as soldiers, all the other rights which have until now been male privileges. It would have to bring about a drastic desegregation of all spheres of social life and dismantle traditional institutions which embody the inequality between the sexes.

One wonders if a desegregated society, where formerly secluded women have equal rights not only economically but sexually, would be an authentic Muslim society.

The Roots of the Modern Situation

What was, and is still, at issue in Morocco is not an ideology of female inferiority, but rather a set of laws and customs which insure that women's status remains one of subjugation. Prime among these are the family laws based on male authority. Although many institutions were withdrawn from the control of religious law (business contracts for example), the family never was. The seventh century laws of the family, based on male authority, were reenacted in modern legislation. The 1957 *Code du Statut Personnel*[1] (which includes all laws relating to the family) is no more than a brilliant transposition of Imam Malik's graceful and anecdotal *al-Muwatta*[2] into a series of articles, sections and sub-sections in the concise Napoleonic tradition.

Since male modernists have recognized the necessity of altering the sexes' division of labor, and since heads of Arabo-Muslim states have affirmed their condemnation of sexual inequality, it seems appropriate to inquire how, and with what consequences, the emerging desire for sexual equality will be met in modern Arabo-Muslim societies.

In fact, the problem seems to be insoluable. The fate of women's liberation is directly linked to the political and economic conflicts which are tearing apart modern Muslim societies. Every political setback generates a new necessity to liberate all the forces for development in Islamic nations. But, paradoxically, every political setback inflicted by infidels generates an antithetical necessity to re-affirm the traditional Islamic nature of these societies as well. In a single blow, both the forces for modernity and the forces for tradition are unleashed, and they then confront each other with dramatic consequences for the relation of sexes.

Let us examine more closely how this conflict works itself out symbolically in matters of policy in Morocco. Morocco claims to be modern, Arab and Muslim. Each one of the three adjectives — modern, Arab and Muslim — refers to a complicated nexus of needs and aspirations, more often contradictory than complementary, which gives the modern Muslim way of life a powerful impetus and a specific character.

For example, Morocco as a modern state is a member of the United Nations and signed the *Declaration of Human Rights* which stipulates, in Article 16 concerning family regulations, that:

> Men and women, regardless of race, nationality or religion, having reached the age of puberty, have the right to marry and establish families. They have equal rights with regard to marriage, in the marriage, and in the event of its dissolution.

However, as a Muslim society affirming its will to keep the family under traditional Muslim law, Morocco promulgated a modern code which respects dutifully, whenever possible, the seventh century *Sharia* ("divine law"). Article 12, for example reestablishes the traditional institution of guardianship, according to which it is not the woman who gives herself in marriage, but a male guardian who gives her to her husband:

> The woman does not, herself, conclude the marriage act, but should have herself represented by a *wali* [guardian] whom she designates for this purpose.

Article 11 stipulates that the *wali* should be a male. Another glaring violation of the *Declaration of Human Rights* is Article 29 which forbids a woman to choose a husband from outside the Muslim community. But the marriage of a Muslim man to a non-Muslim woman is not forbidden. The differences in the sexes' rights and duties towards each other in marriage are so extreme that they are stated in two different articles: Article 35, "The Rights of the Wife towards her Husband" and Article 36, "The Rights of the Husband towards his Wife."

The actual situation in modern Muslim Morocco will appear incoherent to anyone looking for the secure and comforting logic of Cartesian "rational behavior." But if we discard childish frames of mind and try to grasp the complexity of a situation where individuals act and reflect on their actions, responding to the disconcerting demands of the world around them, what seems incoherent becomes intelligible in its existential context. This approach is particularly important in the analysis of male-female dynamics in modern Morocco where the hopes, fears and expectations of men and women are, more than ever, numerous and contradictory. I will scrutinize three of the imperatives of modern Muslim life which have immediate bearing on the family structure and the sexes' relations before looking at the historical sources of modern legislation.

1. The need for sexual equality: the Muslim male feminist movement as an effort to change the sexual division of labor.
2. The need to be Arab: Arab nationalism as a survival reflex in the face of Western domination.
3. The need to be Muslim: religion as the comfortable cradle of a cosmic ideology.

THE NEED FOR SEXUAL EQUALITY

The feminist movement is an expression and a byproduct of Arabo-Muslim nationalism. Kacem Amin (1863-1908) and Salama Musa (1887-1958) consider the liberation of the woman as a condition *sine qua non* for the liberation of Arabo-Muslim society from the humiliating hegemony of the West. By liberation of the woman they mean a total equality with men in all spheres of social life. In 1955, Salama Musa in his book, *The Woman is Not a Man's Toy*,[3] dismissed the Western example of women's liberation as a particularly misleading one because it does not, according to him, elevate the woman from the status of a female to the status of a human being. He urged his society to turn instead towards China and other Asian nations as better models of liberation. But I am not so much interested here in the content of the feminist movement's program as in its genesis and causality, in its instrumental aspect as part of the strategy for liberation.

A prime characteristic of Arabo-Muslim society is its obsession with the West and the West's power to dominate others.

> Easterners and Westerners differ in many things...Among their differences is the fact that Westerners, in general, dominate the Easterners and take away from them their cotton, their rubber, their copper, their oil. And they beat them whenever they try to rebel.[4]

One of the pillars of Western domination, according to the feminists, is its productiveness.

> Production in Europe and the U.S.A. is considerable and this is due to the fact that in those countries both men and women are involved in the process of production.[5]

Consequently, one of the causes of Muslim weakness is the fact that only half of the nation works and produces. The other half, the women, are prevented from taking part in production:

> Among the weaknesses in a society is the fact that the majority of its members are not involved in a productive work process...Women in every society average half of the population. To condemn them to be ignorant and inactive occasions the loss of half of the society's productive potential and creates a considerable drain upon the society's resources.[6]

Therefore to educate women and prepare them to take part in the production is a necessity if the East is to rival the West in power and productivity. Kacem Amin dismisses as idiotic theories according to which women do not have the same capacity and the same intelligence as men. He affirms that, "If men are superior to the woman in regard to physical strength and intelligence, it is due to the fact that men were engaged in work activities which brought them to use their brain and body and therefore to develop them."[7] He argues that when women are given the same opportunities the differences will disappear quickly.

But to include women in education and production implies sexual desegregation, and in 1895 many believed this to be against Islam and its laws:

> Many people still believe that to educate the women is not necessary. They go even as far as to think that to teach the woman how to read and write is against the *Sharia* and a violation of the divine order.[8]

Kacem Amin tries to show that the woman's seclusion and her exclusion from social affairs was not due to Islam but to secular customs "which prevailed in nations conquered by Islam and did not disappear with Islam's teaching."[9] He affirms that those secular traditions were reenforced by reactionary, secular political regimes throughout the Muslim nations' history. Therefore, to change institutions which coerce women into seclusion and ignorance is not in any way an attack on or a violation of Islam. In Kacem Amin's argument, Islam becomes the most liberating of religions towards women:

> Muslim law, before any other legal system, legalized woman's equality with men and asserted their freedom and liberty at the times when women were still in the most debased condition in all the nations of the world. Islam granted her all human rights and recognized her legal capacity, equal to that of men in all matters...[10]

When the traditionalists set out to prove the opposite, they had a rather easy task. Sheikh Ibn Murad, in a sweeping attack against a Tunisian modernist who wrote a book asserting that the liberation of the woman does not contradict Islam, labeled the modernist an agent of Catholic priests paid to destroy Muslim society.[11] He proceeded to establish that, indeed, Islam believes in sexual inequality.

> The meaning of marriage is the husband's supremacy...Marriage is a religious act...which gives the man a leading power over the woman for the benefit of humanity.[12]

In this century the husband's supremacy has been seriously undermined by the effects of modernization which has gradually thrust women out of their homes and into classrooms, offices and factories,. Although sexual desegregation in Morocco is slow and was for decades solely and upperclass urban process, it nevertheless affected the society's sexual balance seriously enough to provoke renewed claims that Islam and its laws are the everlasting guiding light in sexual matters.

THE NEED TO BE ARAB

The need to reaffirm the essentially Arab nature of the society, with Islam as the source of the society's ideals, is dismissed as unimportant by some theoreticians of modernization. Daniel Lerner, for example, makes his task as a social scientist rather simple. After first equating modernization with Westernization, he affirms that Westernization is sweeping Bagdad and Cairo.

> Underlying the ideologies there pervades in the Middle East a sense that old ways must go because they no longer satisfy the new wants...Where Europeanization once penetrated only the upper level of Middle East society, affecting mainly leisure-class fashions, modernization today diffuses among a wider population and touches public institutions as well as private aspirations with its disquieting 'positivist spirit'.[13]

Daniel Lerner was writing these sentences in 1958, two years after the Anglo-French-Israeli attack on the Egyptian nation, at a time when demonstrations in Iraq, Syria, Jordan, Lebanon, Lybia, Tunisia, Morocco, Bahrein, Qatar, Kuwait and Aden affirmed their sympathy with Egypt as an aggressed-upon Arab nation. If Lerner had listened for fifteen minutes to any Arabo-Muslim radio station in the Mediterranean, he probably would have given more credit to the ''underlying ideologies,'' and accorded more importance to the itchy ambivalence the word ''Europeanization'' provokes in both the ''leisure-class'' and ''the wider population.'' Fortunately for social science, he noticed that ''a complication in Middle East modernization is its own ethnocentricism—expressed politically in extreme nationalism, psychologically in passionate xenophobia.''[14]

But I believe Arabo-Muslim ethnocentricity, dismissed by Lerner as a complication, is one of the most meaningful features of modernization. Being Arab and being Muslim in modern Morocco influences both institutions and sexual interaction.

A peculiar feature of the concept of being Arab is that many people and many nations who never thought of themselves as Arab are claiming to be so since the Second World War. Nowadays being Arab is primarily a political, not a racial, claim. According to Anouar Abdel-Malek, Egyptians before the 1930's took great pride in being Egyptians, the inheritors of the civilization of the ancient pharoahs, and they emphasized their difference from Arabs.[15] The predominantly Berber origin of the Moroccan population is no secret and was used for demagogic purposes by the French colonizers interested in aggravating any indigenous divisions. The division between ''Berbers'' and ''Arabs'' was a handy one.[16] But many countries, like Egypt and Morocco, found they needed to unite as Arabs in the face of Western domination. This they did, in their distress, under the banner of Arab nationalism.

The political and cultural meaning of being Arab is clearly expressed in Allal al-Fasi's analysis of the options opened to Morocco in the 1940s:

> Morocco must, in order to live and prosper, join a bloc of nations. Two such blocs are open for her choosing: the French Union, whose form has not yet crystallized, and the Arab Union, which has become an actual reality. In the promised French Union,

Morocco will find herself—judging from past experience—in the utmost difficulties, because there is a conflict of interests and beliefs between her and France...Morocco is convinced that she would not be happy within this colonial union, but would remain as a storehouse for raw material and as a hatching ground for soldiers to serve France. Morocco's adherence to the Arab Union, on the other hand, would bring Morocco within this Eastern family, to which she has belonged for ten centuries and from which she had been excluded for reasons beyond her control...[17]

In 1945, the Arab character of Morocco was far from being evident, and Allal al-Fasi had to plead his cause to persuade the first members of the League[18] to define Arab in such a way that even not-so-Arab Morocco could fit the definition.[19]

History has proved Allal al-Fasi to be correct in his predictions. His party's wishes became those of the Moroccan state. Morocco, as an independent nation, became a member of the Arab League on October 1, 1958. It affirmed its Arab identity in the *Loi Fondamentale de Royaume* (June, 1961) which became the basis of the 1962 Constitution.

Article 1, Morocco is an Arab and a Muslim country.

Article 2, Islam is the official religion of the State.

Article 3, The Arabic language is the official and national language of the State.

THE NEED TO BE MUSLIM

Morocco by affirming its claim to be Arab and Muslim expressed a view of the world based on specific aspirations and drawing its ideology from specific sources. If to be Arab implies a political and cultural choice, to choose to be Muslim implies a particular cosmic vision of the world and a specific organization of institutions in general and of the family in particular. Islam is not merely a religion. Islam is a holistic approach to the world, characterized by a rather:

unique insistence upon itself as a coherent and closed system, a sociologically and legally and even politically organized entity in the mundane world and an ideologically organized entity as an ideal.[20]

We will see now what being Muslim implied for the Moroccan family.

In the seventh century, Mohammad created the *Umma* concept. There was nothing familiar about it in the minds of his contemporaries, deeply rooted in their tribal allegiances. He had to transfer the believers' allegiance from the tribe, a biological group with strong totemic overtones, to the Umma, a sophisticated ideological group based on religious belief.[21] Islam transformed a group of individuals into a community of believers. This community is defined

xiv

by characteristics which set the relations of the individuals within the *Umma* both to each other and to non-believers:

> In its internal aspect, the *Umma* consists of the totality of individuals bound to one another by ties, not of kinship or race, but of religion, in that all its members profess their belief in the one God, Allah, and in the mission of his prophet, Muhammad. Before God and in relation to Him, all are equal without distinction of rank, class or race...In its external aspect, the *Umma* is sharply differentiated from all other social organizations. Its duty is to bear witness to Allah in the relations of its members to one another and with all mankind. They form a single indivisible organization, charged to uphold the true faith, to instruct men in the ways of God, to persuade them to the good and to dissuade them from evil by *word and deed*.[22]

One of the devices the Prophet used to implement the *Umma* was the creation of the institution of the Muslim family which was quite unlike any existing sexual unions.[23] Its distinguishing feature was its strictly defined monolithic structure.

Because of the novelty of the family structure in Mohammad's revolutionary social order, he had to codify in detail its regulations. Sex is one of the instincts whose satisfaction was regulated at length by the religious law during the first years of Islam. The link in the Muslim mind between sexuality and the *Sharia* has shaped the legal and ideological history of the Muslim family structure[24] and consequently of the relation between the sexes. One of the most enduring characteristics of this history is that the family structure, because divine, is assumed to be unchangeable.

The controversy has raged throughout this century between traditionalists who claim Islam prohibits any change in the sexes' roles, and modernists who claim that Islam allows for the liberation of women, the desegregation of society and the equality of the sexes. But both factions agree on one thing: Islam should be kept as the sacred basis of the society. In this book I want to demonstrate that there is a fundamental contradiction between Islam as interpreted in official policy and equality of the sexes. Sexual equality violates Islam's premise, actualized in its laws, that the heterosexual love is dangerous to Allah's order. Muslim marriage is based on male dominance. The desegregation of the sexes violates Islam's ideology on the woman's position in the social order': the woman should be under the authority of fathers, brothers or husbands. Since she is considered by Allah to be a destructive element, she is to be spatially confined and excluded from matters other than those of the family. The woman's access to non-domestic space is put under the control of males.

Paradoxically, and contrary to what is commonly assumed, Islam does not advance the thesis of women's inherent inferiority. Quite the contrary, it

xv

affirms the potential equality between the sexes. The existing inequality does not rest on an ideological or biological theory of women's inferiority, but is the outcome of specific social institutions designed to restrain her power: namely, segregation and legal subordination of the woman to the man in the family structure. Nor have these institutions generated a systematic and convincing ideology of women's inferiority. Indeed, it was not difficult for the male-initiated and male-led Feminist movement to affirm the need for woman's emancipation, since traditional Islam recognizes equality of potential. The democratic glorification of the human individual, regardless of sex, race or status, is the kernel of the Muslim message.

In Western culture, sexual inequality is based on belief in women's biological inferiority. This explains some aspects of Western women's liberation movements, such as that they are almost always led by women, that their effect is often very superficial, and that they have not yet succeeded in changing significantly the male-female dynamics in that culture. In Islam there is no such belief in female inferiority. On the contrary, the whole system is based on the assumption that the woman is a powerful and dangerous being. All sexual institutions (polygamy, repudiation, sexual segregation, etc.) can be perceived as a strategy for containing her power.

This belief in the woman's potence is likely to give the evolution of the relationship between men and women in Muslim settings an entirely different pattern from the Western one. For example, if there are any changes in the sexes' statuses and relations, they will tend to be more radical than in the West and will necessarily generate more tension, more conflict, more anxiety and more aggression. While the women's liberation movement in the West focuses on the woman and her claim for equality with men, in Muslim countries it would tend to focus on the mode of relatedness between the sexes and thus would probably be led by men and women alike. Because men can see how the oppression of women works against men, women's liberation would assume the character of a generational conflict, rather than a sexual conflict. This could already be seen in the opposition between the young nationalist and the old traditionalists at the beginning of the century, and currently can be seen in the conflict between parents and children over the dying institution of arranged marriage.

At stake in Muslim society is not the emancipation of women (if that only means equality with men), but the fate of the heterosexual unit. Men and women were and still are socialized to perceive each other as enemies. The desegregation of social life makes them realize that besides sex, they can also give each other friendship and love. Muslim ideology, which views men and women as enemies, tries to separate the two, and empowers men with institutionalized means to oppress women. But, while fifty years ago there was coherence between Muslim ideology and Muslim reality as embodied in the family system, now there is a wide discrepancy between that ideology and the reality which it pretends to explain. This book explores many aspects of the discrepancy and describes the *sui-generis* character of male-female dynamics in one of the most striking mixtures of modernity and Muslim tradition: Morocco.

The *Umma* is at the same time a social and religious group, and therefore the problem of the relation between secular and divine power arises. Islam solves it by subordinating unequivocally the secular authority to the religious one and by denying to the secular authority the right to legislate:[25]

> The head of the *Umma* is Allam, and Allah alone. His rule is immediate and his commands, as revealed to Muhammed, embody the Law and Constitution of the *Umma*. Since God is himself the sole Legislator, there can be no room in Islamic political theory for legislation or legislative powers, whether enjoyed by a temporal ruler or by any kind of assembly. There can be no sovereign state, in the sense that the state has the right to enact its own law, though it may have some freedom in determining its constitutional structure. The law precedes the state, both logically and in terms of time, that the state exists for the sole purpose of maintaining and enforcing the law.[26]

In a word, the Muslim's allegiance is not to a secular power, be it the state or its legislators, but to the *Sharia*, which transcends both humanity and temporality. The fact that God is the legislator gives the legal system a specific configuration:

1. It denies the existence of human legislation:

   > strictly speaking, Islamic theory does not recognize the possibility of human legislation and that which the human rules is to make are regulations for carrying the divine law into effect.[27]

2. It asserts the inalterability of the law and its eternal hold on human action:

   > The *Sharia*...is universally accepted as the Law of God. God, at any rate so far as human experience of him may presume to go, is unchanging and to a pious mind this may appear to imply that his law is also unchangeable.[28]

3. It extends the scope of the law to matters which usually belong to other spheres:

   > Law then in any sense in which a Western lawyer will recognize the term, is but part of the whole Islamic system, or rather it is not even a part but one of several inextricably combined elements thereof. *Sharia*, the Islamic term which is commonly rendered in English by 'Law' is rather 'the whole duty of man,' moral

and pastoral theology and ethics, high spiritual aspirations and the detailed ritualistic and formal observance which to some minds is a vehicle for such aspirations and to others a substitute for it, all aspects of law: public and private hygiene and even courtesy and good manners are all part and parcel of the *Sharia*.[29]

Is it correct to say, then, that the Muslim world did not develop a modern legal system in the Western sense of the word? Are the laws governing public and private actions of Muslims today the very laws sketched by Mohhamad? Of course not. The *Sharia* had to confront the daily realities of the increasingly numerous and culturally diverse members of the *Umma*. Schools of law were gradually created and specialists of law appeared. They endeavored to extrapolate and interpret the divine principles in order to meet the earthly needs of the believer in his day-to-day life.

The result was a gradual liberation of some subjects from the hold of the religious law. Joseph Schacht distinguishes two kinds of legal subject matter in Islamic law.[30] First, subject matter upon which the *Sharia* failed to maintain its hold: penal law, taxation, constitutional law, law of war and law of contracts and obligations. Second, subject matter upon which the *Sharia*'s hold was uncontested for centuries and in some areas is uncontested even today: purely religious duties, family law (marriage divorce, maintenance etc.), law of inheritance and law of endowments for religious institutions. These have been and still are, closely connected with religion and therefore are still ruled by the *Sharia*.

Interference by the state in any matter admitted to be within the domain of the *Sharia* presupposes acceptance of the Western idea of sovereign secular power.

Whereas a traditional Muslim ruler must, by definition, remain the servant of the Sacred Law of Islam, a modern government, and particularly a parliament with the modern idea of sovereignty behind it, can constitute itself its master.[31]

Even though impregnated with the Western concept of sovereign secular power, the Muslim *Umma* through the traditionalist supporters of the *Sharia's* sovereignty, strongly resisted the intervention of the modern legislators in family law.

THE HISTORICAL INTERESTS BEHIND MODERN LEGISLATION

Modern legislation in the Muslim world did not spring from any new ideological conception of the individual and society, as had been the case in Mohammad's seventh century revolutionary Muslim order. Modern legislation was initiated and carried out by the colonial powers[32] and after independence was continued by the independent nation states. In both cases, the interests of the individual in general and of women in particular were secondary if not irrelevant compared to the interests of the powers involved.

The colonial powers were motivated to intervene in Muslim legislation, not by idealistic concern for the natives, but by their own economic interests. This was the case of the Anglo-Muhammadan Law in India from 1772 onward and the *Droit Musulman* in Algeria from 1830 onward.

The psychological result of the foreign powers' intervention in Muslim legislation was to transform the *Sharia* into a symbol of Muslim identity and the *Umma's* integrity. Modern changes were identified as the enemy's subtle tools for carrying out the destruction of Islam.

When the Muslim states became independent, modern legislation was still not initiated in the interests of the masses. The new laws were closely connected with the battle between traditional law practitioners and modernists, who were mostly lawyers in the Western sense of the word.[33] It was not only a battle between two different conceptions of law, it was also a clash of interests between two groups of professionals. The new laws forced the traditional "lawyers" to give up some of their power, and their profits, to the young modernist lawyers.

Unlike what happened in China, the Moroccan Nationalist movement never made the transition from an independence movement to a nation-building movement. After having "driven the foreigners out," the Nationalists revealed themselves as unable to transform their ideology and political apparatus into an instrument for social change. According to the Moroccan historian, Abdallah Laroui, the creativity of the Nationalist movement as a producer of ideas for change, died out years before independence. He buries it in 1930-1932.[34] Nor did any other group among those which played important roles in the last eighteen years offer a coherent set of solutions to the country's problems.

The main feature of post-independence policy seems to be impericism, ad hoc decision-making, rather than the subordination of those decisions to a long term program of action.[35] The immediate interests of the independent nation states were the determining factors which motivated the legislators. Their inability to generate a genuine modern ideology made family legislation depend directly on traditional ideologies and contemporary contingencies, whence its inconsistency.[36]

The absence of a genuine modern ideology reenforced the hold of Islam as the only coherent ideology which masses and rulers could refer to. It is therefore not surprising that Morocco, like other independent Muslim states, recognized Islam as the ideology of the family in its otherwise Western-inspired *Code*.

The law of 1957 creating the commission charged with the task of writing a Muslim code was justified thus:

> Considering that the Kingdom of Morocco is going through a period characterized by deep changes in all matters and namely in legislative matters; considering that the Muslim law constitutes an eminently delicate matter susceptible to many interpretations; considering the absolute necessity therefore, to gather the rules of this law into a code so as to facilitate its teaching as well as to facilitate its application . . . have decided on the creation of a commission entrusted with the task of elaborating the Muslim code of personal status.[37]

The *Code du Statut Personnel* stipulates that in all cases which cannot be solved by reference to the *Code*, the source to turn to for guidance is the jurisprudence of the Malekite school.[38] The founder of the Malekite school, Imam Malik Ibn Anas, was an Arab who lived in Medina and was a judge in the eighth century (A.D.). He spelled out in two chapters of his *Muwatta*,[39] one on marriage, the other on divorce, the basis for the institution of the family. There is more than an inspirational similarity between Malik's *Muwatta* and the Moroccan *Code de Statut Personnel*. The idea prevailing in Malik's time that sexuality is a religious matter to be regulated by divine laws seems to be one of the concepts modern legislators did not question at all.

The seventh century concept of sexuality, as embodied in the modern family laws, conflicts dramatically with the sexual equality and desegregation fostered by modernization. In the first part of this book I want to explore, through early Muslim sources, the Muslim ideology of the sexes as it is revealed by the institution of the family. In the second part, I want to analyze, through my data and other sources of information on the present situation, the modernizing trend as embodied in women's gradual acquisition of the right to be educated and compete for jobs. I will look especially closely at the effects of modernization on male-female interaction both within and without the family.

PART I

*The Traditional Muslim
View of Women and Their
Place In The Social Order*

CHAPTER 1

The Muslim Concept of Active Female Sexuality

THE FUNCTION OF THE INSTINCTS

The Christian concept of the individual as tragically torn between two poles
—good and evil, flesh and spirit, instinct and reason—is very different from the
Muslim concept. Islam has a more sophisticated theory of the instincts, more
akin to the Freudian concept of the libido. It views the raw instincts as energy.
The energy of instincts is pure in the sense that it has no connotation of good or
bad. The question of good and bad arises only when the social destiny of men is
considered. The individual cannot survive except within a social order. Any
social order has a set of laws. The set of laws decides what use of the instincts is
good or bad. It is the use made of the instincts, not the instincts themselves,
which is beneficial or harmful to the social order. Therefore, in the Muslim
order it is not necessary for the individual to eradicate his instincts or to control
them for the sake of control itself, but he must use them according to the
demands of the religious law.

> When Mohammad forbids or censures certain human activities, or urges their
> omission, he does not want them to be neglected altogether, nor does he want them to
> be completely eradicated, or the powers from which they result to remain altogether
> unused. He wants those powers to be employed as much as possible for the right
> aims. Every intention should thus eventually become the right one and the direction
> of all human activities one and the same.[1]

For example, aggression and sexual desire, if harnessed in the right direction, serve the purposes of the Muslim order and, if suppressed or used
wrongly, can destroy that very order:

> Muhammad did not censure wrathfulness with the intention of eradicating it as a
> human quality. If the power of wrathfulness were no longer to exist in man, he would
> lose the ability to help the truth to become victorious. There would no longer be holy
> war or glorification of the Word of God. Muhammad censured the wrathfulness that
> is one in God and in the Service of God deserves praise . . .[2]
> . . . Likewise when he censures the desires, he does not want them to be abolished
> altogether, for a complete abolition of concupiscence in a person would make him
> defective and inferior. He wants the desire to be used for permissible purposes to

serve the public interests, so that man becomes an active servant of God who willingly obeys the divine commands.[3]

Imam Ghazali (1050-1111) in his book, *The Revivification of Religious Sciences*,[4] gives a detailed description of how Islam integrated the sexual instinct in the social order and placed it at the service of God. He starts by stressing the antagonism between sexual desire and the social order:

> If the desire of the flesh dominates the individual and is not controlled by the fear of God, it leads men to commit destructive acts.[5]

But used according to God's will, the desire of the flesh serves God's and the individual's interests in both worlds, and enhances life on earth and in heaven. Part of God's design on earth is to insure the perpetuity of the human race, and sexual desires serve this purpose:

> Sexual desire was created solely as a means to entice men to deliver the seed and to put the woman in a situation where she can culitvate it, bringing the two together softly in order to obtain progeny, as the hunter obtains his game, and this through copulation.[6]

He created two sexes, each one of them equipped with a specific anatomic configuration which allows them to complement each other in the realization of God's design:

> God the Almighty created the spouses, he created the man with his penis, his testicles and his seed in his kidneys [Kidneys were believed to be the semen-producing gland.]. He created for it veins and channels in the testicles. He gave the woman a uterus, the receptacle and depository of the seed. He burdened men and women with the weight of sexual desire. All these facts and organs manifest in an eloquent language the will of their creator, and address to every individual endowed with intelligence an unequivocal message about the intention of his design. Moreover, the Almighty God did clearly manifest his will through his messenger (benediction upon him and salute) who made the divine intention known when he said 'Marry and multiply.' How then can man not understand that God showed explicitly his intention and revealed the secret of his creation? Therefore, the man who refused to marry fails to plant the seed, destroys it and reduces to waste the instruments created by God for this purpose.[7]

Serving God's design on earth, sexual desire also serves his design in heaven:

> The sexual desire as a manifestation of God's wisdom has, independently of its manifest function, another function: when the individual yields to it and satisfies it, he experiences a delight which would be without match if it were lasting. It is a foretaste of the delights secured for men in Paradise, because to make a promise to men of delights they have not tasted before would be ineffective . . . This earthly

delight, imperfect because of it being limited in time, is a powerful motivation to incite men to try and attain the perfect delight, the eternal delight and therefore urges men to adore God so as to reach heaven. Therefore the desire to reach the heavenly delight is so powerful that it helps men to persevere in pious activities in order to be admitted to heaven.[8]

Because of the dual nature of the sexual desire (earthly and heavenly) and because of its tactical importance in God's strategy, its regulation had to be divine as well. In accordance with God's interests, the regulation of the sexual instinct was one of the key devices in Mohammad's implementation on earth of a new social order in then pagan Arabia.

FEMALE SEXUALITY — ACTIVE OR PASSIVE?

According to George Murdock, societies fall into two groups with respect to the manner in which they regulate the sexual instinct. One group enforces the respect of sexual rules by a "strong internalization of sexual prohibitions during the socialization process;" the other enforces that respect by "external precautionary safeguards such as avoidance rules" because these societies fail to internalize sexual prohibitions in their members.[9] According to Murdock, Western society belongs to the first group while societies where veiling exists belong to the second.

Our own society clearly belongs to the former category, so thoroughly do we instill our sex mores in the consciences of individuals that we feel quite safe in trusting our internalized sanctions . . . We accord women a maximum of personal freedom, knowing that the internalized ethics of premarital chastity and post-marital fidelity will ordinarily suffice to prevent abuse of their liberty through fornication or adultery whenever a favorable opportunity presents itself. Societies of the other type . . . attempt to preserve premarital chastity by secluding their unmarried girls or providing them with duennas or other such external devices as veiling, seclusion in harems or constant surveillance.[10]

However I think that the difference between these two kinds of societies resides not so much in their mechanisms of internalization as in their concept of female sexuality. In societies where seclusion and surveillance of women prevail, the implicit concept of female sexuality is an active concept; in societies where there are no such methods of surveillance and coercion of the woman's behavior, the concept of female sexuality is a passive concept.

The Muslim feminist Kacem Amin, in his attempt to grasp the logic of woman's seclusion and veiling and the basis of sexual segregation, came to the conclusion that women are better able to control their sexual impulses than men and that consequently sexual segregation is a device to protect men, not women.[11]

He started by asking who is fearing what in such societies. He concluded, from the fact that women do not appreciate seclusion very much and conform to it only because they are compelled to, that what is feared is *fitna*, i.e., disorder, chaos. (*Fitna* also means a beautiful women . . . the connotation of a *femme fatale* attraction which makes men lose their self control. In the way Kacem Amin used it *fitna* could be translated as chaos provoked by sexual disorder and initiated by the woman.) He then asked who is protected by seclusion:

> If what men fear is that women might succumb to their masculine attraction, why did not they institute veils for themselves? Did men think that their ability to fight temptation was weaker than women's? Are men considered less able than women to control themselves and resist their sexual impulse? . . . Preventing women from showing themselves unveiled expresses men's fear to lose control over their minds and fall prey to *fitna* whenever they are confronted with a non-veiled woman. The implications of such an institution lead us to think that women are believed to be better equipped in this respect than men.[12]

Kacem Amin stopped his enquiry here and, thinking probably that his findings were absurd, concluded jokingly that if men are the weak sex, they are the ones who need protection and therefore the ones who should veil themselves.

Why does Islam fear *fitna*? Why does Islam fear the power of female sexual attraction over men? Does Islam assume that the male cannot cope sexually with an uncontrolled female? Does Islam assume that women's sexual capacity is greater than men's?

Muslim society is characterized by a contradiction between what can be called "an explicit theory" and "an implicit theory" of female sexuality and therefore a double theory of the sexes' dynamics. The explicit theory is the prevailing contemporary belief according to which men are aggressive in their interaction with women, and women are passive. The implicit theory is epitomized in Imam Ghazali's classical work.[13] He sees civilization as struggling to contain the woman's destructive, all-absorbing power. Women must be controlled to prevent men from being distracted from their social and religious duties. Society can only survive by creating the institutions which foster male dominance through sexual segregation.

The explicit theory, with its antagonistic, "machismo" vision of the sexes' relationship, is epitomized by Abbas Mahmoud al-Aqqad.[14] In *The Woman in the Quran* Aqqad attempts to describe the male-female dynamic as it appears through the Divine Book. Aqqad opens his book with the quotation of the Quran establishing the fact of male supremacy ("the men are superior to them by a degree'') and deduces hastily that "the message of the Quran which makes men superior to women is the manifest message of human history, the history of Adam's descendants before and after civilization."[15]

What Aqqad finds in the Quran and in human civilization is a complementarity between the sexes based on their antagonistic natures. The characteristic of the male is the will to power, the will to conquer. The characteristic of the female is a negative will to power. All her energies are vested in wanting to be conquered, in wanting to be overpowered and subjugated. Therefore, "She can only expose herself and wait while the man wants and seeks."[16]

Although Aqqad has neither the depth nor the brilliant systematic deductive approach of Freud, his ideas on the male-female dynamic are very similar to Freud's emphasis on the "law of the jungle" aspect of sexuality. The complementarity of the sexes, according to Aqqad, resides in their antagonistic wills and desires and aspirations:

> Males in all kinds of animals are given the power — embodied in their biological structure — to compel females to yield to the demands of the instinct (that is, sex) . . . There is no situation where that power to compel is given to the women over the men.[17]

Like Freud, Aqqad endows the woman with a hearty appetite for suffering. Women enjoy surrender.[18] More than that, for Aqqad, woman's pleasure and happiness are experienced only in her subjugation, her defeat by the male. The ability to experience pleasure in suffering and subjugation is the kernel of femininity, which is masochistic by its very nature. "The woman's submission to the man's conquest is one of the strongest sources of woman's pleasure . . ."[19] The "machismo" theory casts the man as the hunter and the woman as the prey. This vision is widely shared and deeply ingrained in both men's and women's vision of themselves.

The implicit theory of female sexuality, as seen in Imam Ghazali's interpretation of the Quran, casts the woman as the hunter and the man as the passive victim. The two theories have one component in common, the woman's *qaid* power ("the power to deceive and defeat men, not by force, but by cunning and intrigue"). But while Aqqad tries to link the female's *qaid* power to her weak constitution, the symbol of her divinely-decreed inferiority, Imam Ghazali sees her power as the most destructive element in the Muslim social order.

The whole Muslim organization of social interactions and spacial configurations can be understood in terms of the woman's *qaid* power. The social order then appears as an attempt to subjugate her power and neutralize its disruptive effects. The opposition between the implicit and the explicit theories in Muslim society would appear clearly if I could contrast Aqqad and Imam Ghazali. But, whereas the implicit theory is brilliantly articulated in the systematic work of Imam Ghazali on the institution of marriage in Islam, the explicit theory has an unfortunate advocate in Aqqad whose work is an amateurish mixture of history, religion, his own brands of biology, and anthropology. I shall therefore contrast Imam Ghazali's conception of sexual dynamics not with Aqqad's but with that of another theoretician, one who is not a Muslim but who has the advantage of possessing a machismo theory which is systematic in the elaboration of its premises — Sigmund Freud.

IMAM GHAZALI VS. FREUD: ACTIVE VS. PASSIVE

To contrast Freud and Imam Ghazali we are faced with a methodological obstacle, or rather what seems to be one. When Imam Ghazali was writing the chapter on marriage in his book, *The Revivification of Religious Sciences,* in the eleventh century, he was endeavoring to reveal the true Muslim belief on the subject. This is not so for Freud who was endeavoring to build a scientific theory with all that the word ''scientific'' implies of objectivity and universality. Freud did not think that he was elaborating a European theory of female sexuality; he thought he was elaborating a universal explanation of the human female. But this methodological obstacle is easily overcome if we are ''conscious of the historicity of culture.''[20] We can view Freud's theory as a ''historically defined'' product of his culture. Linton noticed that anthropological data has shown that it is culture which determines the perception of biological differences and not the other way around:

> All societies prescribe different attitudes and activities to men and to women. Most of them try to rationalize these prescriptions in terms of the physiological differences between the sexes or their different roles in reproduction. However, a comparative study of the statuses ascribed to women and men in different cultures seems to show that while such factors may have served as a starting point for the development of a division, the actual prescriptions are almost entirely determined by culture. Even the psychological characteristics ascribed to men and to women in different societies vary so much that they can have little physiological basis.[21]

A social scientist is in a biographically determined situation where he finds himself ''in a physical and socio-cultural environment as defined by him, within which he has his position, not merely his position in terms of physical space and outer time or of his status and role within the social system but also his moral and ideological position''[22] and so we can consider Freud's theory of sexuality in general, and of female sexuality in particular, as a reflection of his society's beliefs concerning the question and not as a scientific (i.e., objective and ahistorical) theory. Therefore by comparing Freud and Imam Ghazali's theories, we will be comparing the different conceptions of sexuality of the two different cultures.

The novelty of Freud's contribution to Western contemporary culture, is his acknowledgment of sex as the very source of civilization (when sublimated, of course). The rehabilitation of sex as the foundation of civilized creativity led him to the reexamination of sex differences. This reassessment of the differences and of the consequent contributions of the sexes to the social order yielded the concept of female sexuality in Freudian theory which interest us here.

In analyzing the differences between the sexes, Freud was struck by a peculiar phenomenon — bisexuality — which is rather confusing to anyone trying to assess sex differences rather than sex similarities:

> Science next tells you something that runs counter to your expectations and is probably calculated to confuse your feelings. It draws your attention to the fact that portions of the male sexual apparatus also appear in women's bodies, though in an atrophied state and vice-versa in the alternative case. It regards their occurence as indications of bisexuality as though an individual is not a man or a woman but always both — merely a certain amount more one than the other.[23]

The deduction one expects from bisexuality is that anatomy cannot be accepted as the basis for sex differences. Freud made this deduction:

> You will then be asked to make yourself familiar with the idea that the proportion in which masculine and feminine are mixed in an individual is subject to quite considerable fluctuations. Since, however, apart from the very rarest cases, only one kind of sexual product, ova or semen, is nevertheless present in one person, you are bound then to have doubts as to the decisive significance of those elements and must conclude that what constitutes masculinity or femininity is an unknown characteristic which anatomy cannot lay hold of.[24]

Where then did Freud get the basis for his polarization of human sexuality into a masculine sexuality and a feminine sexuality, if he affirms that anatomy cannot be the basis of such a difference? He explains this in a footnote, apparently considering it a very secondary point:

> It is necessary to make clear that the conceptions ''masculine'' and ''feminine'' whose content seems so unequivocal to the ordinary meaning, belong to the most confused terms in science and can be cut up into at least three paths. One uses masculinity and femininity at times in the sense of activity and passivity, again in the biological sense and then also in the sociological sense. The first of these three meanings is the essential one and the only one utilizable in psychoanalysis.[25]

The polarization of human sexuality into two kinds, feminine and masculine, and their equation with passivity and activity in Freudian theory helps us to understand Imam Ghazali's theory which is characterized precisely by the absence of such a polarization. It conceives of both male and female sexuality partaking of and belonging to the same kind of sexuality.

For Freud, the sex cells' functioning is symbolic of the male-female relation during intercourse. He views it as an antagonistic encounter between aggression and yielding:

> The male sex cell is actively mobile and searches out the female and the latter, the ovum, is immobile and waits passively . . . This behavior of the elementary sexual organism is indeed a model for the conduct of sexual individuals during intercourse. The male pursues the female for the purpose of sex union, seizes hold of her and penetrates into her.[26]

For Imam Ghazali, both the male and female have an identical cell. The word sperm (*Ma'*, "water drop") is used for the female as well as for the male cell. Imam Ghazali referred to the anatomic differences between the sexes when he was clarifying Islam's position concerning coitus interruptus (*'azl*), a traditional method of birth control practiced in pre-Islamic times. In trying to establish the prophet's position on *'azl*, Imam Ghazali portrayed the Muslim theory of procreation and consequently, the sexes' contribution to it and their respective roles in it:

> The child is not created from the man's sperm alone, but from the union of a sperm from the male with a sperm from the female . . . and in any case the sperm of the female is a determinant factor in the process of coagulation.[27]

The puzzling question is not why Imam Ghazali failed to see the difference between the male and female cell, but why Freud, who was more than knowledgeable about biological facts, saw the ovum as a passive cell whose contribution to procreation was minor compared to that of the sperm. In spite of their technical advancement, European theories clung for centuries to the idea that the sperm was the only determining factor in the procreation process; babies were prefabricated in the sperm[28] and the uterus was just a cozy place where they developed.

Imam Ghazali's emphasis on the identity between male and female sexuality appears clearly in his granting the female the most uncontested expression of phallic sexuality, namely ejaculation. This reduces the differences between the sexes to a simple difference of pattern of ejaculation, the female's ejaculation being much slower than the male's:

> The difference in the pattern of ejaculation between the sexes is the source of hostility whenever the man reaches his ejaculation before the woman . . . The woman's ejaculation is a much slower process and during that process her sexual desire grows stronger and to withdraw from her before she reaches her pleasure is harmful to her.[29]

Here we are very far from the bedroom scenes of Aqqad and Freud which sound like battle fields rather than shelters of pleasure. In Imam Ghazali, there is neither aggressor nor victim, there are only two people cooperating to give each other pleasure.

The recognition of female sexuality as active is an explosive acknowledgment for the social order with far-reaching implications for its structure as a whole. But denying the identity between male and female sexuality is also an explosive and decisive choice. For example, Freud recognizes that the clitoris is an evident phallic appendage and that consequently the female is more bisexual than the male.

> There can be no doubt that the bisexual disposition which we maintain to be characteristic of human beings manifests itself much more plainly in the female than in the male. The latter has only one principal sexual zone — only one sexual organ — whereas the former has two: the vagina, the true female organ and the clitoris, which is analogous to the male organ.[30]

Instead of elaborating a theory which integrates and elaborates the richness of both sexes' particularities, however, Freud elaborates a theory of female sexuality based on reduction: the castration of the phallic assets of the female. A female person, bisexual in infancy, develops into a mature female only if she succeeds in renouncing the clitoris, the phallic appendage:

> The elimination of the clitoral sexuality is a necessary pre-condition for the development of femininity.[31]

The pubertal development process brings atrophy to the female body while it enhances the phallic potential of the male's, thus creating a wide discrepancy in the sexual potential of humans, according to their sex:

> Puberty which brings to the boy a great advance of libido, distinguishes itself in the girl by a new wave of repression which especially concerns the clitoral sexuality. It is a part of the male sexual life that sinks into repression. The reenforcement of the inhibitions produced in the woman by the repression of puberty causes a stimulus in the libido of the man and forces it to increase its capacity; with the height of the libido, there is a rise in the over-estimation of the sexual, which can be present, in its full force only when the woman refuses and denies her sexuality.[32]

The female child becomes a woman when her clitoris "acts like a chip of pinewood which is utilized to set fire to the harder wood."[33] Freud adds that this process takes some time during which the "young wife remains anesthetic."[34] This anesthesia may become permanent if the clitoris refuses to give up its excitability. The Freudian woman, faced with her phallic partner, is therefore predisposed to frigidity:

> The sexual frigidity of women, the frequency of which appears to confirm this disregard (the disregard of nature for the female function) is a phenomenon that is still insufficiently understood. Sometimes it is psychogenic and in that case accessible to influence; but in other cases it suggests the hypothesis of its being constitutionally determined and even of being a contributory anatomical factor.[35]

By contrast with the passive frigid Freudian female, the sexual demands of Imam Ghazali's female appear truly overwhelming, and the necessity for the male to satisfy them becomes a compelling social duty:

> The virtue of the woman is a man's duty. And the man should increase or decrease sexual intercourse with the woman according to her needs so as to secure her virtue.[36]

The Ghazalian theory directly links the security of the social order to that of the woman's virtue, and thus to the satisfaction of her sexual needs. Social order is secured when the woman limits herself to her husband and does not create *fitna* or chaos by enticing other men to illicit intercourse. The awe of the acknowledgment of the overpowering sexual demands of the active female appears when Imam Ghazali admits how difficult it is for a man to satisfy a woman:

> If the prerequisite amount of sexual intercourse needed by the woman in order to guarantee her virtue is not assessed with precision, it is because such an assessment is difficult to make and difficult to satisfy.[37]

He cautiously ventures to suggest that the man should have intercourse with the woman as often as he can, once every four nights if he has four wives. He suggests this as the extreme limit, otherwise the woman's sexual needs might not be met:

> It is just for the husband to have sexual intercourse with his wife every four nights if he has four wives. It is possible for him to extend the limit to this extreme. Indeed, he should increase or decrease sexual intercourse according to her own needs.[38]

Freud's and Ghazali's stands on forepleasure are directly influenced by their visions of female sexuality. For Freud, the emphasis should be on the coital act which is primarily "the union of the genitals",[39] and he deemphasizes forepleasure as on the borderline between normal (genital) union and perversion, which consists:

> . . . in either an anatomical transgression of the bodily regions destined for sexual union or a lingering at the intermediary relations to the sexual object which should normally be rapidly passed on the way to definite sexual union.[40]

In contrast, Imam Ghazali recommends forepleasure, acknowledged as primarily in the interest of the woman, as a duty for the believer. Since the woman's pleasure necessitates a lingering at the intermediary stages, the believer should strive to subordinate his own pleasure which is served mainly by the genital union:

> The Prophet said, 'No one among you should throw himself on his wife like beasts do. There should be, prior to coitus, a messenger between you and her.' People asked him, 'What sort of messenger?' The Prophet answered, 'Kisses and words.'[41]

The Prophet indicated that among the things which would constitute a weakness in a man's character would be that:

> . . . he will approach his concubine-slave or his wife and that he will have intercourse with her without having prior to that been caressing, been tender with her in words and gestures and laid down beside her for a while, so that he does not harm her, by using her for his own satisfaction, without letting her get her satisfaction from him.[42]

THE FEAR OF FEMALE SEXUALITY

The perception of female aggression is directly influenced by the theory of her sexuality. For Freud the female's aggression, in accordance with her sexual passivity, is turned inward. She is masochistic:

> The suppression of woman's aggressiveness which is prescribed for them constitutionally and imposed on them socially favors the development of powerful masochistic impulses, which succeed, as we know, in binding erotically the destructive trends which have been diverted inwards. Thus masochism as people say, is truly feminine. But if, as happens so often, you meet with masochism in men, what is left for you but to say that these men exhibit very plainly feminine traits.[43]

The absence of active sexuality molds the woman into a masochistic passive being. It is therefore no surprise that in the actively sexual Muslim female aggressiveness is seen as turned outward. The nature of her aggression is precisely sexual. The Muslim woman is endowed with a fatal attraction which erodes the male's will to resist her and reduces him to a passive acquiescent role. He has no choice; he can only give in to her attraction, whence her identification with *fitna*, chaos, and with the anti-divine and anti-social forces of the universe:

> The Prophet saw a woman. He hurried to his house and had intercourse with his wife Zaynab, then left the house and said, "When the woman comes towards you, it is Satan who is approaching you. When one of you sees a woman and he feels attracted to her, he should hurry to his wife. With her, it would be the same as with the other one."[44]

Commenting on this quotation, Imam Muslim, an established voice of Muslim tradition, the Prophet was referring to the:

> . . . fascination, to the irresistible attraction to women God instilled in man's soul, and he was referring to the pleasure man experiences when he looks at the woman, and the pleasure he experiences with anything related to her. She resembles Satan in his irresistible power over the individual.[45]

This attraction is a natural link between the sexes. Whenever a man is faced with a woman, *fitna* might occur:

> When a man and a woman are isolated in the presence of each other, Satan is bound to be their third companion.[46]

The most potentially dangerous woman is one who has experienced sexual intercourse. It is the married woman who will have more difficulties in bearing sexual frustration. The married woman whose husband is absent is a particular threat to men:

> Do not go to the women whose husbands are absent. Because Satan will get in your bodies as blood rushes through your flesh.[47]

In Moroccan folk culture this threat is empitomized by the belief in Aicha Kandisha, a repugnant female demon. She is repugnant precisely because she is libidinous. She has pendulous breasts and lips and her favorite pastime is to assault men in the streets and in dark places, to induce them to have sexual intercourse with her, and ultimately to penetrate their bodies and stay with them forever.[48] They are then said to be inhabited. The fear of Aicha Kandisha is more than ever present in Morocco's daily life. The fear of the castrating female is a legacy of tradition.

Moroccan folk culture is permeated with a negative attitude towards femininity. Loving a woman is popularly described as a form of mental sickness, a self-destructive state of mind. As the Moroccan proverb says,

> Love is a complicated matter
> If it does not drive you crazy, it kills you.[49]

The best example of this distrust of women is the sixteenth century poet, Sidi Abderahman El Mejdoub. His rhymes are so popular they have become proverbs.

> Women are fleeting wooden vessels
> Whose passengers are doomed to destruction.

or:

> Don't trust them [women] so you would not be betrayed
> Don't believe in their promises so you would not be deceived
> To be able to swim, fish need water
> Women are the only creatures who can swim without it.[50]

and finally:

> Women's intrigues are mighty
> To protect myself I never stop running
> Women are belted with serpents
> And bejeweled with scorpions.[51]

The Muslim order faces two threats: the infidel without and the woman within.

The Prophet said, 'After my disappearance there will be no greater source of chaos and disorder for my nation than women.'[52]

The irony is that Muslim and European theories come to the same conclusion — the woman is destructive to the social order: for Imam Ghazali, because she is active; for Freud, because she is not.

Different social orders have integrated the tensions between religion and sexuality in different ways. For example, in the Western Christian experience, it was sexuality itself which was attacked, degraded as animality and condemned as anti-civilization. The individual was split into two antithetical selves: the spirit and the flesh; the ego and the id. The triumph of civilization implied the triumph of soul over flesh, of ego over id, of controlled over uncontrolled, of spirit over sex.

Islam took a substantially different path. What is attacked and debased is not sexuality; it is the woman who is attacked as the embodiment of destruction, the symbol of disorder. She is *fitna*, the polarization of the uncontrollable, a living representative of the dangers of sexuality and its rampant disruptive potential. We have seen that the Muslim theory of instincts considers raw instinct as energy which is likely to be used constructively for the benefit of Allah and his society if one lived according to his laws. Sexuality *per se* is not a danger. On the contrary, it has three positive, vital functions. It allows the believers to perpetuate themselves on earth, a rather indispensable condition if the social order is to exist at all. It serves as a "foretaste of the delights secured for men in Paradise,"[53] thus encouraging men to strive for paradise and to obey Allah's rule on earth. The third function is the role of sexual satisfaction as necessary to intellectual effort.

The Muslim theory of sublimation is entirely different from the Western Christian tradition as represented by Freudian psychoanalytic theory. Freud views civilization as a war against sexuality.[54] Civilization is sexual energy "turned aside from its sexual goal and diverted towards other ends, no longer sexual and socially more valuable."[55] The Muslim theory views civilization as the outcome of satisfied sexual energy. Work is not the result of sexual frustration; it is the result of a contented sexuality of a harmoniously-lived sexuality:

The soul is usually reluctant to carry out its duty because duty [work] is against its nature. If one puts continuous pressures on the soul in order to make it do what it loathes, the soul rebels. But if the soul is allowed to relax for some moments by the means of some pleasures, it fortifies itself and becomes after that alert and ready for work again. And in the woman's company, this relaxation chases sadness and pacifies the heart. It is advisable for the pious souls to divert themselves by means which are religiously lawful."[56]

According to Ghazali, the most precious gift God gave humans is reason. Its best use is in the search for knowledge. To know the human environment, to know the earth and galaxies etc., is to know God. Knowledge (science) is the best form of prayer for a Moslem believer. But to be able to devote his energies to knowledge, man has to reduce the tensions within and without his body, avoid being distracted by external elements, and avoid indulging in earthly pleasures. The woman is a dangerous distraction which must be used for the specific purpose of providing the Muslim nation with offspring and quenching the tensions of the sexual instinct. But the woman should not, in any way, be an object of emotional investment or the focus of attention, which should all be devoted to Allah alone in the form of knowledge-seeking, meditation and prayer.

Ghazali's conception of the individual's task on earth is enlightening in that it reveals that, in spite of the beauty of the Muslim message, it considers humanity to be constituted by males only. Women are considered not only outside of humanity but a threat to it as well. The Muslim wariness of heterosexual involvement is embodied in sexual segregation and its corollaries: arranged marriage, the important role of the mother in the son's life, and the fragility of the marital bond (as revealed by the institutions of repudiation and polygamy). The whole Muslim social structure can be seen as an attack on, and a defense against, the disruptive power of female sexuality.

CHAPTER 2

The Regulation of Female Sexuality in the Muslim Social Order

It is a widely shared belief among historians in different cultures that human history is progressive, that human society, in spite of accidents and setbacks, moves progressively from "savagery" to "civilization." Islam, has a progressive vision of history. The year 622, the *Hijra,* is the year one of civilization. Before the *Hijra* was the *Jahiliya,* the time of barbarism, the time of ignorance.[1] Islam maintains that one of the dimensions of society where there was progress is human sexuality.[2] Promiscuous, lax and uncontrolled in the *Jahiliya,* sexuality under Islam is described by contrast as obeying rules. The specific, unique code of Islam's law outlaws fornication as a crime. But what is peculiar about Muslim sexuality as a civilized sexuality is this fundamental discrepancy: if promiscuity and laxity are signs of a barbarism, then the only sexuality civilized by Islam is the woman's sexuality; the man's sexuality is promiscuous (by virtue of polygamy) and lax (by virtue of repudiation).[3] This contradiction is evident in both the seventh century family legislation and the modern Moroccan Code.

POLYGAMY

Decree No. 2-57-1040 of August 1957 charged a commission of ten men with the elaboration of a Muslim Moroccan code of law, the *Code de Statut Personnel.* These ten men reenacted polygamy, whose basis is the famous verse[3] of Surah I, the only mention of polygamy in the whole Quran:

> Marry of the women, who seem good to you, two, three, or four, and if ye fear that ye cannot do justice [to so many] then one [only] . . .

A notable peculiarity of the verse is that the only condition limiting a man's right to polygamy is fear of injustice, a subjective feeling not easy to define legally. The Moroccan legislators, probably aware of the rather outmoded aspect of polygamy, rephrased Verse Four in such a way that the word "forbidden" closely follows "polygamy," but the content is identical:

> Art. 30: If injustice is feared, polygamy is forbidden.

The Koran does not provide a justification for polygamy, but Ghazali does. According to him, polygamy's basis is instinctual. Ghazali's justification reveals clearly the flaw in the Muslim theory of sexuality, and provides us with one of the most revealing insights into the problem which modern Morocco, as a Muslim society, is obliged to solve. Polygamy entitles the male not simply to satisfy his sexuality, but to indulge it to saturation without taking into consideration the woman's needs, the woman being considered a simple "agent" in the process:

> Once the agent [the sexual excitation] is known, the remedy should be adapted to its intensity and degree, the aim being to relieve the soul from tension. One can decide for greater number [of women] or lesser number . . . for the man burdened with a strong sexual desire and for whom one woman is not enough to guarantee his chastity [chastity for a married person being abstention from *zina,* from fornication], it is recommended that he add to the first wife, others. The total should not exceed, however, four.[4]

Polygamy implies that a man's sexual drive might require copulation with more than one partner in order to relieve his soul (and body) from sexual tensions. Ghazali implies elsewhere that there is no difference in the nature of male and female sexual drives. Thus he unintentionally acknowledges a latent reason for women's reluctant attitude towards the Muslim order.

Men and women are considered to have similar instinctual drives, yet men are entitled to as many as four partners in order to satisfy those drives, while women must content themselves with at most one man and sometimes as little as a quarter of one. Since saturation of the sexual impulse for males requires polygamy, one can speculate that fear of its inverse — one woman with four husbands — might explain the assumption of women's insatiability, which is at the core of the Muslim concept of female sexuality. Since Islam assumes that a sexually frustrated individual is a very problematic believer and a troublesome citizen of the *Umma*, the distrust of women is even greater.

Polygamy also has a psychological impact on the self-esteem of men and women. It enhances men's perception of themselves as primarily sexual beings and emphasizes the sexual nature of the conjugal unit. Moreover, polygamy is a way for the man to humiliate the woman as a sexual being; it expresses her inability to satisfy him. For Moroccan folk wisdom, this function of polygamy as a device to humiliate the woman is evident:

> Debase a woman by bringing in [the house] another one.[5]

The verse justifying polygamy in the Koran also gives, without any condition or limit, the right to possess as many concubines as "your right hand possess." But the Moroccan legislators, taking into account the budgeting difficulties of the contemporary believer, do not say anything about the institution of concubinage which died out in Morocco with the disappearance of female slavery at the beginning of the twentieth century. (My grandmother was kidnapped in

Chaouia Plain, sold in Fez, and bore my mother as a concubine to a member of the landowning urban bourgeoisie, then politically and financially powerful. This group was the main buyer of female slaves for decades after the French occupation in 1912.)

REPUDIATION

Though polygamy is mentioned only once in the Quran, repudiation is the subject of long, detailed and numerous verses. The most commonly referred to is Surah II:

Verse 227: And if ye decide upon Divorce [remember that]Allah is hearer, knower.

Verse 229: Divorce must be pronounced twice, and then a woman must be retained in honor or released in kindness.

But legally speaking the most significant reference to the institution of repudiation is probably Verse 20 of Surah IV which reveals the basic amateurishness of the male decision to sever the marital bond:

And if ye wish to exchange one wife for another and ye have given into one of them a sum of money (however great) take nothing from it.

The words ''wish'' and ''exchange'' are the key elements in the Muslim phenomenon of verbal repudiation whose characteristic is the unconditional right of the male to break the marriage bond without any justification, and without having his decisions reviewed by a court or a judge. In reenacting the seventh century institution, the Moroccan Code limits the judge's role to simply registering the husband's decision:

Art. 46: Repudiation can be performed either verbally or in writing, or by signs and gestures if the husband is an illiterate man, deprived of the speech capacity.

Art. 80: The *adouls* [Muslim court officials] issue a repudiation act as soon as they are asked to do so.

Like polygamy, repudiation has an instinctual basis, but while polygamy deals with the intensity of the male's sexual drive, repudiation deals with its instability. Repudiation prevents the male from losing his sexual appetite through boredom. It aims at insuring a supply of new sexual objects to protect the man against the temptation of *zina*:

If God by his goodness and his grace facilitates man's life [by allowing him to be polygamous] and that man attains thus the peace of heart by them [women], that is good. If not, the changing process is recommended.[6]

This recommendation is enforced by exemplary men such as Hassan, the Prophet's grandson:

It has been said that Hassan Ibn Ali was a marriage addict. He married 200 wives. Sometimes he'd marry four at a time; sometimes he'd repudiate four at a time and marry new ones. Mohammad (upon him benediction and *salut*) said to Hassan, 'You resemble me physically and morally' . . . It has been said that this proclivity to marry often is precisely one of the similarities between Hassan and the messenger of God (upon him benediction and *salut*).[7]

The somewhat ridiculous aspect of repudiation did not escape Allah himself who warned the believer entrusted with the verbal power to break the marital bond not to make "the revelations of Allah a laughingstock [by your behavior]."[8]

The right to polygamy and repudiation granted exclusively to the male seems to have been an innovation in seventh century Arabia. Historical evidence indicates that marriage patterns had been more varied and less codified then. Some forms of marriage imply that the woman had a right to self-determination in choosing a husband or dismissing him. Indeed, the Prophet himself, despite his powerful attraction as a triumphant military leader and successful statesman, was himself faced with female sexual self-determination. He was asked in marriage by many women and he was rejected, literally repudiated, by many as well.

The Prophet's life is not a simple historical document in Islam. The detailed record of his thoughts and deeds is, after the Quran which is the word of God, the prime source of the teachings which shape and guide the believer's life. The Prophet's life is an example of how a Muslim should deal with and find solutions to his daily problems. It is the guiding light for facing obstacles and resolving them according to the Muslim ideal.

THE PROPHET'S EXPERIENCE
OF FEMALE SELF-DETERMINATION

The Prophet's marital life seems to be symbolic of the transition Arabia was undergoing. He lived for 62 years (born in 570 AD of the Christian calendar, died in 632). He married for the first time in the year 595 and with his first wife, Khadija, had a monogamous marriage which lasted 25 years, until her death in 620. It was only then that the Prophet started a new marital life, where in a span of twelve years (620-632) he married twelve women, arranged three other marriages which did not take place, and rejected several female suitors who asked for his hand, or rather "offered themselves," according to the consecrated Muslim formula.[9]

The first woman who asked him in marriage was his first wife, Khadija Bint Khuwalid, a wealthy and active Quraichi woman who invested her fortune in the trade operations then flourishing in Mecca. She employed Muhammad's services to accompany one of her trading caravans and was so impressed by his trustworthiness that she decided to marry him. He was then twenty-five years old, and it was his first marriage. She was forty years old, and it was her third. She bore him all his children (four daughters and two sons who died young) except Ibrahim, the son of Maria, the Copt concubine.[10]

Among the women who offered themselves to the Prophet are Umm Sharik, whose proposal he did not accept, and Leila Bint Al Khatim whose proposal he did accept. The latter marriage did not take place because Leila was discouraged by her tribe. Her people convinced her that her proud temperament was ill-suited for the accommodations a harem requires.

The lack of ritual around such a move on the part of the woman is illustrated by the dialogue between the Prophet and Leila:

> She came to the Prophet (upon him Allah's peace and prayer) who was sitting talking to another man, and who did not see her coming, until he felt her hand on him. He said, 'Who are you?' She said, 'I am Leila Bint Al Khatim. I came to you to offer myself. Will you marry me?' He said, 'I accept.'[12]

For a woman to decide to initiate a sexual union seems to have been a casual gesture made by the woman only, to the exclusion of her father or male relatives. Although Leila's kin discouraged her marriage, they did so not as authorities, but as persuasive counselors, worried about her well-being. She decided not to marry the Prophet not because she was coerced, but because she was convinced by their argument concerning the Prophet's other wives and her inability to cope with them.

Hiba ("the act by which a woman gives herself to a man,") was outlawed after the Prophet died.[13] If he was the last Arab man to be chosen freely by women, he was also probably the last to be repudiated by women.

There were several women with whom the Prophet contracted marriages but did not consummate them.[14] In three cases the marriage was broken by a repudiation formula pronounced by the woman. Some reports say that the formula was repeated three times by the woman. (This makes it look identical to the repudiation formula which was institutionalized by Islam as a man's privilege: if the man pronounces it three times, the divorce is definite; if he pronounces it once or twice only, the marital bond is suspended for some weeks, after which the husband can resume his marriage.)

Every time the formula was pronounced by the woman, the Prophet covered his face with his sleeve, left the nuptial room and asked for the woman to be returned to her tribe immediately. It appears that repudiation, like *hiba,* was characterized by a lack of ritual which leads me to think that it was a rather common happening.

When she [Asma Bint An Numan] entered the room where he [the Prophet] was, he closed the door and released the curtain. When he thrust his hand towards her, she said, 'I take refuge in Allah from thee.' The Prophet immediately covered his head with his sleeve and said, 'You are granted such a protection,' three times. He then left her and gave orders for her to be returned to her tribe.[15]

Similar indicents happened with Mulaika Bint Ka'ab and Fatima Bint Ad-Dahhak.[16]

Muslim sources give many versions of the motives which led the three women to behave the way they did. The most common explanation of their behavior is that the three of them, who all belonged to tribes different from that of the Prophet, were deceived by their co-wives.[17] The Quraichi wives of the Prophet (led of course by Aicha, the indefatigable, vivacious beloved of the Prophet) threatened by the three tribal women's beauty and exoticism, instructed the newcomers to pronounce the formula "so that the Prophet would love them more." Victims of deceit, according to these versions, the three tribal women were surprised to see the Prophet's reaction.

I think these rather heavy-handed versions of the story are the work of Muslim historians who thought it necessary to disguise the fact that the Prophet was rejected and "repudiated". One of the reports says explicitly that the woman rejected the prophet because she did not like him.[18] This is a much more likely reason. At least two of the women, Asma and Mulaika, were famous for their beauty.[19] They were young. The Prophet was in his early sixties, and, a very important point, he was polygamous. For women like Asma, who was herself from a princely tribe[20], the Prophet's prestige as a leader would not make him very desirable if all he had to give her was shared with more than nine colleagues. But, in any case, the explanation of their behavior is secondary here. What we are interested in is the fact that, in the Prophet's time, there was a customary formula by which a woman could dismiss her husband. The Prophet's phobic behavior (having to leave her immediately) after the woman pronounced the formula shows that this was so.

If a woman could dismiss her husband at will, then she possessed a substantial amount of independence and self-determination. The Muslim social order was vehemently opposed to self-determination for women and declared that only men could repudiate their spouses.

The fear of female self-determination is basic to the Muslim order and is closely linked to the fear of *fitna*. If women are not constrained then men are faced with an irresistable sexual attraction which inevitably leads to *fitna* and chaos. The Prophet's own experience of the overwhelming attraction of female sexuality underlies much of the Muslim attitude towards women and sexuality.

THE PROPHET'S EXPERIENCE OF THE IRRESISTIBLE ATTRACTION OF WOMEN

The Prophet's interactions with women, his intimate quarrels with his wives, his behavior with the women he loved, are the basis for many legal features specific to the Muslim family structure. One of the striking aspects of his interaction with women is the contradiction between the ideals he set up as a model for Muslim believers to follow when dealing with women and the way he actually dealt with them himself. One of those ideals is what should motivate a man to marry:

> The Prophet said that the woman can be married for her religion [Muslim faith], for her fortune, or her beauty. Be motivated in your choice by her religion.[21]

Although many of his marriages were motivated by religious and political ones (politics after all is religion in Islam), such as the need for tribal alliances, many of his marriages were motivated solely by the woman's beauty.

His marriage with the Jewess, Safiya Bint Huyay, could not possibly have been motivated by the need for an alliance, the Jews being his defeated enemies at the time. Moreover, when Safiya was captured by Muslim soldiers after the defeat of her people, it was not evident that she was, as part of the booty, going to fall into Mohammad's share, the booty being shared according to the democratic, customary rules of Arab Razzia. One report mentions that actually Safiya was allotted to a soldier called Dahia but that when the Prophet heard about her "incomparable beauty" he sent for Dahia, paid him Safiya's price and freed her before marrying her.[22]

His marriage with another Jewish woman, Rayhana Bint Zayd, could not have been motivated by alliance either. Like Safiya, she belonged to a Jewish tribe, was captured after her people's defeat, and was known to be "a beautiful woman."[23] But unlike Safiya her marital status is contested; some reports say that she was kept as a concubine and never became a wife of the Prophet.

Maria the Copt, a famous beauty, was given as a gift from Egypt to the Prophet.[24] He had intercourse with her as a concubine, and she bore him a son, Ibrahim, who died in infancy. The Prophet's attraction for Maria was so strong that it led him to violate another of his ideals: the justice a man should realize in his dealings with his wives. A man should keep strictly to the rotation schedule and not have intercourse with a wife, even if he so desired, if it was not her day. The Prophet was caught by one of his wives, Hafsa, having intercourse with Maria in Safiya's room and on Safiya's day. "Oh Prophet of God, in my room and on my day," fulminated Safiya angrily. Afraid of the anger of his other wives and mainly of his most beloved Aicha, he promised Hafsa never to touch

Maria again if she kept the incident secret.[25] She did not and he received orders from God to free himself from his promise and resumed intercourse with Maria.[26] Maria's power over the Prophet is best described in Aicha's words:

> I never was as jealous as I was of Maria. That is becuase she was a very beautiful, curly-haired woman. The Prophet was very attracted to her. At the beginning, she was living near us and the Prophet spent entire days and nights with her until we protested and she became frightened.[27]

The Prophet decided then to transfer her to a more secure dwelling far from his legitimate wives, and kept seeing her in spite of their pressure.

Another woman the Prophet married for her beauty, although in this case alliance was a motive as well, was Juwariya Bint Al Harith who was, according to Aicha's description, ''so beautiful that whoever caught a glimpse of her fell in love with her.''[28] According to Aicha, the main motive of the Prophet's marriage to Juwariya was physical attraction:

> The Prophet was in my room when Juwariya came to ask him about a contract. By God, I hated her when I saw her coming towards him. I knew that he was going to see what I saw [i.e., her beauty].[29]

Another instance of the effect of female beauty on the Prophet is that of Dubaa Bint Amr who ''was among the most beautiful of Arab women . . . Her hair was long enough to cover all her body.''[30] The Prophet heard about her beauty, went to her son and asked him if he could marry his mother. The son, following the custom in such instances, told the Prophet that he would have to ask his mother's opinion. He did, and she was so excited about the prospect of such a union that she told her son he should have given her in marriage right away, that it was impolite of him to have put a condition to the Prophet's legitimate desire. But when the son went to the Prophet with the hope that the subject of his mother would be discussed, the Prophet never brought it up again. He had heard meanwhile that she was indeed beautiful, but that she also was aging.

But the most significant example of women's irresistible power over the Prophet is probably his sudden (and scandalous by his own people's standards) passion for Zainab Bint Jahch,[31] the wife of his adopted son, Zaid. In Mohammad's Arabia, the link created by adoption was considered identical with ties created by blood. Moreover, Zianab was the Prophet's own cousin, and the Prophet himself had arranged her marriage with his adopted son.

One morning Mohammed went to his adopted son's house to inquire for him, when he saw Zainab, who was half dressed, he felt an irresistible passion for her. She had hurried to the door to let the Prophet know that her husband was not in. She was surprised to see him refuse her invitation to come in, and then ran out grumbling prayers. When she reported the incident to her husband, he went to his adopted father to say that he was ready to divorce Zainab if the Prophet wanted to marry her. The Prophet refused Zaid's proposition until God revealed his order to Mohammad to marry Zainab:

> . . . And thou didst hide in thy mind that which Allah was to bring to light, and thou didst fear mankind whereas Allah had a better right that thou shouldst fear Him. So when Zeyd had performed the necessary formality [of divorce] from her, We have her unto thee in marriage, so that [henceforth] there may be no sin for believers in respect to wives of their adopted sons, when the latter have performed the necessary formality [of release] from them. The commandment of Allah must be fulfilled.[32]

To calm the scandalized clamour of the Prophet's contemporaries, the Muslim God made a lasting change in the institution of adoption. Verse four of Surah XXXIII denied that adoption creates legal and affinal ties between individuals. Article 83 of the Moroccan *Code* reenacted the Quran's decision: "Adoption confers neither legal status nor the rights of parenthood."

One should note here that the Muslim Prophet's heroism consists precisely in his humanity and not in any Quixotic attempt to transcend his limitations. He achieved his colossal task on earth, not because he was outstandingly tough and strong, but because he was vulnerable and able to recognize his vulnerability, acknowledge it and take it into account. The most striking example of this is his acknowledgment of his overwhelming love for Aicha who was not yet eighteen years old when he died in his sixties.

> The Prophet was striving to achieve justice between his wives in whatever he gave them and he respected dutifully the rotation system [one night each], but he used to say, 'God, this is as far as I can go in controlling my inclinations. I have no power over what you own and I don't [meaning heart].' Aicha was the one he loved the most and all his other wives knew that.[33]

The power of women over men has dictated many of the Muslim laws concerning marriage. Men have a right to sexual satisfaction from their wives so that they will be less vulnerable to the attraction of other women. And women must be sexually satisfied so that they do not try to tempt other men.

THE NEED TO INSURE SEXUAL SATISFACTION

Sexual satisfaction for both partners is seen as necessary to prevent adultery. For example *muhsan*, which means "to protect", legally means both "marriage" and "chastity" because a married person should be "protected" from adultery by satisfying his desires within the marriage. Under penal law, the *muhsan* receives a harsher punishment than an unmarried person who has sexual intercourse.[35]

The word *"zina"* means illicit intercourse — "any sexual intercourse between two persons who are not in a state of legal matrimony or concubinage."[36] *Zina* covers both fornication (involving unmarried people) and adultery (involving at least one married individual a *muhsan*). Before Islam, *zina* was not considered a sin, a crime against religion. With Islam it became a crime against God and his laws and order.

Zina was one of the practices the new Muslim recruits were required to renounce. The ritual by which new female converts were admitted into the Muslim community was a pledge to respect the six demands known as the woman's oath of allegiance:

> O Prophet! If believing women come unto thee, taking oath of allegiance unto thee that they (1) will ascribe nothing as partner unto Allah, and will (2) neither steal, (3) nor commit zina (4) nor kill their children, (5) nor produce any lie that they have devised between their hands and feet, (6) nor disobey thee in what is right, then accept their allegiance and ask Allah to forgive them. [numbers mine][37]

As a protective device against *zina,* marriage is highly recommended to believers of both sexes. A sexually frustrated member of the community is considered dangerous. This is the main reason why Islam is opposed to asceticism and requires believers with pious and saintly vocations to acquire pious wives. Abstinence and celibacy are vehemently discouraged.[38] Atika Bint Zaid, a woman who decided to live as a celibate after her husband's death, was discouraged from doing so by the Muslim Caliph Omar, who went so far as to propose marriage to her.[39]

Islam socializes sexual intercourse through the institution of marriage within the framework of the family. The only legitimate sexual intercourse is between married people. Marriage should guarantee sexual satisfaction for husband and wife and protect both partners against seeking satisfaction outside of it. The institution of marriage penalizes the wife or the husband who fails to provide sexual services for the others.

If the wife refuses to have intercourse with her husband she is penalized both on earth and in heaven. The Prophet, according to Imam Bukhari, said a woman "who is asked by her husband to join him in bed and refuses to do so is condemned by the angels who throw anathema on her until the daybreak."[40] Although having swarms of angels set against one is a rather unsettling thought, the most efficient device for bringing the woman to respond sexually to her husband is a material one. Muslim law grants the husband whose wife refuses his advances the right to withhold maintenance from her (food, clothing and lodging) which it is normally his duty to provide. The 1958 Moroccan law safeguards this right for male citizens:

Article 123: The non-pregnant woman who abandons the conjugal community or refuses to have sexual intercourse with her husband may retain her right to maintenance but the judge has the right to suspend her right to maintenance if he commands the woman to return to the conjugal abode or to regain the conjugal bed and she refuses to obey. She has no right of appeal against the judge's decision as long as she does not execute his order.

The availability of sexual intercourse is vital to the man's protection against *zina* because, as we have seen from the Prophet's example, the only way to resist another woman's illicit attraction is to rush to your wife.

This need to protect the man is probably the reason why, even though menstruation is defined as polluting,[41] a husband is allowed to approach his menstruating wife so long as he can avoid penetration. Imam Ghazali explains that the husband can ask his wife to cover her body between the navel and the knee with a cloth and to masturbate him with her hands.[42]

Parallel to the protection of the man against his wife's whimsical or biological obstacles, there exist many legal devices to insure the woman's sexual satisfaction by her husband. Although the right of the woman to ask the judge to pronounce a divorce is limited to a very few grounds, sex is one of them. The woman has the right to ask the judge to initiate a divorce if she can testify that her husband is impotent. While Malik decided that the woman should wait one year before asking for a divorce on the grounds of impotence,[43] the modern Moroccan legislators think it an urgent matter and urge the judge to respond immediately by releasing the woman if she files for divorce on these grounds.[44]

Another form of divorce justified by the lack of sexual satisfaction is *ila*. If the husband makes an oath to abstain from having sexual intercourse with his wife for four months and if he keeps his oath, she can demand a divorce from the judge.[45] The Moroccan *Code* reenacted the *ila* in Article 58.

The compelling duty to provide sexual satisfaction is intelligble only if one is reminded of the fear of unrestrained female sexuality. Curbing active female sexuality, preventing female sexual self-determination, is the basis of many of Islam's family institutions.

REMNANTS OF PRE-MUSLIM SEXUAL PRACTICES

Two techniques of divorce which have survived in Muslim marriages are reminiscent of female self-determination under the *Jahilya* although now the woman's power to dissolve her marriage is subordinated to the judge's decision and approval. The two techniques are *tamlik* and *khul'* , both of which can be considered as survivals of, or transitional compromises with the woman's former freedom in marriage contracts.

The techniques of *tamlik* confer upon the wife the power to divorce her husband if he delegates such power to her. The repudiation formula, "I divorce thee," becomes, "I divorce thee whenever thee decides it."

Imama Malik explains the logic of such a technique: "If a man gives his wife the right to self-determination (*Malaka Amraha*) whatever she decides becomes legally binding."[46] If she decides to leave him, there is nothing he can do about it. He recounts the dialogue between a Muslim judge and a Muslim husband painfully surprised to see his wife use the power he had delegated to her.

> The man: I gave my wife the right to self-determination and she divorced me. What do you think?
> The judge: I think that what she did is perfectly legal.
> The man: Please do not do that [i.e., agree with her against me].
> The judge: I did not do that, you did it.[47]

The *tamlik* technique was not reenacted in 1958 Moroccan *Code*, which specifies that "repudiation subordinated to a condition is valueless."[48] The *tamlik* had subordinated repudiation to the wife's approval. The technique of *tamlik* is interesting because of the mechanisms and concepts involved in it, especially the concept of self-determination as something which can be transferred from the man to the woman. It expressed the idea that the woman's freedom of decision is not an inseparable privilege of the husband, but can be the object of bargaining between the spouses.

Khul' means literally "to cast off." Here it refers to the husband renouncing his rights over the woman as a wife after she has agreed to pay him a certain sum of money to buy her freedom. Imam Malik mentions that it was practiced in the Prophet's time.[49] The buying of the woman's freedom, is often used in cases where it is evidently the woman's fault that the marriage is not functioning. A price is negotiated between the husband and the woman's family and is paid to the unlucky husband.

Schacht sees in *khul'* "an exchange of assets."[50] It seems to be a fair practice by which everybody got something: the woman her freedom and the man a compensation for his loss. But it is easy to imagine the corruption of such a practice into a weapon to oppress the woman. If she has a fortune of her own or comes from a wealthy family, the man may make life so miserable for his wife that she will have to "buy herself off" from him.

Such cases must have been quite frequent because Malik warns that if it is established that the woman was coerced by her husband, the judge should free her and the husband should not be granted indemnization.[51] The Moroccan *Code* institutionalizes the *khul'* technique in Articles 58 and 61. Article 63 warns that, ''The husband shall acquire compensation only if the wife has consented to obtain her divorce without coercion or constraint.''

Tamlik and *khul'* are remnants of women's sexual self-determination before Islam. But most other features of pre-Muslim sexual practices were stamped out by the rules regulating Muslim marriages. For example, before Islam women frequently remarried as soon as they were divorced. If pregnant by their first husband, the child belonged to the second husband.[52] Physical paternity was considered unimportant. Under Islam physical paternity was considered essential, so women are forbidden to remarry until several months had passed and it became evident that they were not pregnant by their previous husband.

IDDA: THE MUSLIM GUARANTEE OF PATERNITY

One of the first affirmations of physical paternity in Arabia was the proverb, ''the child belongs to the bed,'' which is a succinct statement of the Muslim belief. The man who impregnates the woman is the father, not the woman's second husband even if she has remarried.

The idea that a woman impregnated by a believer would engage in intercourse with another believer, even within the frame of marriage, became a blasphemous thought:

> Whoever believes in Allah and in the other world, would not allow his sperm to water another man's child.[53]

Therefore, a woman who is pregnant is forbidden to enter into a new marriage until she gives birth to the child.

> . . . For those [women] with child; the waiting period shall be till they bring forth their burden.[54]

Islam insured physical paternity by instituting the *Idda* period which obliges a widowed or a divorced woman to wait several menstrual cycles before getting married again.[55] Widows are required to wait four months and ten days before marrying again. The divorcée should wait four months.

The Moroccan *Code* reenacts the *idda* just as it was established in the Quran and adopted by Malik. Article 72 forbids a pregnant woman to marry before her child's birth. Article 73 obliges the repudiated wife to wait three consecutive menstrual flows before engaging in a new marital union. But further measures are taken, in specific cases, to prevent any loopholes in the system of paternity.

Even menopausal women cannot go unchecked. On the off chance that they can still conceive, they have to wait three months before seeking a new husband (Article 73). Given the volatile tendencies of marriage markets in Muslim society and their competitiveness (due precisely to repudiation, which liberates a greater number of marriageable women than demography alone would), the *idda* constitutes a rather harsh penalty for all newly divorced women and for menopausal women in particular who have the further disadvantage of being middle-aged.

The penalizing aspect of the *idda* appears even more clearly in the case of women whose menstrual flow is irregular or who do not have a flow at all. On this point there is a significant difference between the Quran and the leader of the school of the Malikites. The Moroccan *Code* emulates the latter. While the Quran requires only a three-month waiting period of those "who despair of menstruation"[56] or have doubts about its regularity, Imam Malik penalizes those two groups with a waiting period of twelve months.[57] Article 73 of the Moroccan *Code* also stipulates that, "women whose menstrual flow is late or irregular, or who can not distinguish between one menstrual flow and the following should wait an *idda* period of twelve months."

The revolutionary new social structure of Islam was based on male dominance. Polygamy, repudiation, the prohibition of *zina* and the guarantees of physical paternity were all designed to foster the transition from a family based on female self-determination to a family based on male control. The Prophet saw the establishment of the male-dominated Muslim family as crucial to the establishment of Islam. He bitterly fought existing sexual practices where marital unions for both men and women were numerous and lax.

CHAPTER 3

The Regulation of Sexuality
in the Pre-Muslim Social Order

MARRIAGE IN EARLY ISLAM

The marriage patterns of the earliest Muslim communities throw a good deal of light on the sexual patterns prevailing in pre-Muslim Arabia at that time. One source of data on marriage in early Islam is the eighth volume of the *Kitab at-Tabaqat al-Kubra* (*"The Book of the Big Classes"*) by Ibn Saad.[1] The work as a whole is a classification of the early Muslim community. The eighth volume, *On Women*, is a compilation of biographical information about the first women converts who formed the Prophet's entourage. The first part of the book contains information on women related to the Prophet either by blood or by affinal ties: his female cousins, his aunts, his daughters and his wives. The second part is a compilation of biographical notices on roughly 574 women who were the first converts.

A systematic analysis of Ibn Saad's book was undertaken in 1939 by Gertrude Stern in order to assess marriage in the early Muslim community[2]. She did not try to interpret her findings or make them fit a particular theory. Her work is therefore a mere description of the marriage processes: betrothal, consent, guardianship, dowry, adultery and the dissolution of marriage ties. She found no "fixed institution of marriage." She describes the existence of a diversity of sexual unions whose "outstanding feature appears to be the looseness of marriage ties in general and the lack of any legal system for regulating procedure."[3]

> If one takes into consideration the preceding facts in conjunction with other factors such as the absence of any contract or legal guardian, the exclusion of the wife from her husband's inheritance, the easy methods of divorce, the lack of a period of seclusion after divorce and widowhood — the *idaa* — the conclusion must be reached that there was no fixed institution of marriage and that marriage ties were in no sense regarded as binding.[4]

The work of Gertrude Stern impresses the reader by its rigorous attempt at objectivity limited to a strict analysis of the data, yet her assertion that "there was no idea of a fixed institution of marriage" can be misleading. It can mean either that there was no fixed institution of marriage at all or that there was no institution of marriage similar to Muslim marriage. The difference is enormous. If she meant to dismiss as irrelevant sexual unions which were not similar to the Muslim one, she was following the Prophet policy of condemning as *zina* all marriages which were not like his ideal.

> . . . it is very probable that Muhammad employed the term *zina* to the very loose matrimonial bonds and the consequent abuses thereof rather than to adultery in the strict sense of the word.[5]

From her description it seems likely that what she meant by "the absence of a fixed institution of marriage" was the absence of a fixed institution similar to Muslim marriage.

According to the biographical data, polygamy did not exist either in Mecca, a sophisticated urban center with trading relations reaching deep into the Byzantine world, or in Medina, the basically agrarian community to which the Prophet emigrated.

> There is no reliable evidence of the practice of polygamy in pre-Islamic times at Al-Madinah [Medina], as understood in the Islamic era, that is, the system of a man marrying a number of women and maintaining them in one or more establishments . . . Moreover, from a study of the genealogical tables which I have compiled, it is to be observed that there is no indication of a well-defined system of polygamy.[6]

She arrived at identical conclusions for Mecca adding:

> It is possible that Meccan men contracted marriages with tribal women, but that they were either of a temporary character or the woman remained with her own people, but as is the case of the *Medinians,* there is no evidence of a man supporting and maintaining more than one wife at a time.[7]

Here Gertrude Stern draws attention to a vital detail usually overlooked in the analysis of pre-Islamic marriages: the uxorilocal charactor of the marriage. Polygamy in an uxorilocal setting is an altogether different institution from polygamy in a virilocal one. Polygamy in an uxorilocal setting could very well co-exist with a similar polyandrous right of the woman who will be visited by many men. It has different implications for the woman's status and sexual freedom than the virilocal Muslim polygamy.

The Prophet's great-grandfather, Hashim, contracted an uxorilocal marriage. The offspring of the union, the Prophet's grandfather, Abd Al Muttalib, was raised by his mother.[8] Hashim contracted the union during a trip to the town of Medina (he was from Mecca), where he asked Salama Bint Amr for her hand and married her. She bore him Abd Al Muttalib. Hashim left Medina and went back to Mecca, leaving the child behind with its mother. After Hashim's death, his brother went to Medina to fetch the boy, then an adolescent. It took three days of negotiations between Salama and the uncle to decide the fate of the child who said that he would not leave his mother unless she ordered him to do so. Salama is described as a woman who:

> . . . because of her noble birth and her high position among her people, never allowed herself to marry anyone except under the condition that she would be her own master and retain the initiative to leave the husband if she disliked him.[9]

Muslim historians link sexual self-determination to a high position of the woman. It is very understandable that Ibn Hisham, the historian of the *Sira* (''biography'') of the Prophet, thought of finding a justification other than matriliny to explain Salama's attitude, since matriliny was condemned as prostitution by the time of the *Sira's* writing.

The prophet's own father, Abdallah, contracted a matrilineal marriage with Amina Bint Wahb:

> When Abdallah Ibn Abd Al Muttalib married Amina Bint Wahb, he stayed with her three days. Such was the prevailing custom when the man decided to marry a woman who stayed among her own tribe.[10]

Amina evidently stayed with her own kin. When Abdallah died on his way back to Mecca from a trip, Amina was seven months pregnant with the Prophet. The child stayed with his mother until her death. He was then six years old. Only after her death was he taken in charge by his father's kin.[11]

The woman's independence from her husband and her insistence on sexual self-determination seems to have been possible only because she was backed by her own people. This independence persisted even with the growing affirmation of patrilineal trends in the Arab society of Mohammad's time when the principle of marriage by capture or purchase was gaining ground.

Marriage by capture or purchase implies a structure of virilocal polygamy. This was a novel idea in the Prophet's time as is evidenced by his own inconsistent attitude towards it. Although he himself married thirteen women, he adamantly opposed Ali, his son-in-law, when the latter decided to contract a second marriage and thus provide Fatima, the Prophet's favorite daughter (who was not particularly known for her beauty) with an unwelcome co-wife.

> I will not allow ʿAli Ibn Abi Taleb and I repeat, I will not allow Ali to marry another woman except under the condition that he will divorce my daughter. She is a part of me, and what harms her, harms me.[12]

The Prophet appears to have known that it was a harmful arrangement for a woman to share a husband. Another illustration is provided by the Ansar, the Prophet's political supporters. They thought polygamy so degrading that they urged one of their daughters, Leila Bint Al Khatim, not to marry the Porphet.[13] They argued that she was too proud. She might get jealous and create troubles in the household of the Prophet and thus provoke tensions between him and his allies. A third example is that of the Prophet's wife (or concubine) Rayhana who is supposed to have been divorced by him once because she was too jealous to bear sharing him with her co-wives. He married her again when she regained control over her feelings.[14] But probably the most outstanding instance of rebellion against polygamy is that of Amina, the Prophet's great grand-daughter. Whenever she contracted a marriage she insisted on keeping total control over the marriage. Before marrying Zayd Ibn Omar she set the condition that:

> He will not touch another woman. He will not prevent her from spending his money, and will not oppose any decision she might make. Otherwise she will leave him.[15]

WOMEN'S RESISTANCE TO ISLAM

Amina recognized that women were much happier before the Prophet's time. When asked why she was so funny and humorous and her sister, Fatima, so deadly serious, she answered,

> It is because she [Fatima] was named after her Muslim grandmother [Fatima is the daughter of the Prophet] while I was named after my pagan great great grandmother, who died before Islam's arrival. [Amina is the mother of the Prophet.][16]

This idea is corroborated by historical incidents, some violent and bloody like the so-called Harlots of Hadramaut, and others more peaceful like the insistence of early Moslem women on their freedom of action concerning the initiation and the ending of sexual unions.

After the death of the Prophet in June 632, a vast movement of apostasy swept the Arab peninsula, and the tribes refused to pay taxes to the Prophet's successor, the first Caliph Abu Bakr.[17] The movement was severely repressed and ended one year later after fierce battles between Islam and its opponents. One of the movements of apostasy was led by a group of women who celebrated in a joyful atmosphere the death of the Prophet. The event is recorded in Ibn Habib Al Bagdadi's *Kitab al-Muhabbar*[18]

> There were in Hadramaut six women, of Kindah and Hadramaut, who were desirous for the death of the Prophet of God; they therefore [on hearing the news] dyed their hands with henna and played on the tambourine. To them came out the harlots of Hadramaut and did likewise so that some twenty-odd women joined the six.[19]

The Caliph received two letters relating the event and asking the Caliph to punish the blasphemous women. Both letters were written by men. The

Caliph's answer to his governor over Kindah, giving orders to retaliate, reads as follows:

In the name of God, the compassionate, the Merciful. From Abu Bakr to Al Muhagir Ibn Abi Umayyah. The two righteous servants [of God] who remained steadfast in their religion when the greater part of their tribes apostasized (may God grant them the reward of the righteous for this and smite the others with the fate of the wicked), have written to me declaring that before them there are certain women of the people of Yemen who have desired the death of the Prophet of God, and that these have been joined by singing-girls of Kinda and prostitutes of Hadramaut, and they have dyed their hands and shown joy and played on the tambourine in defiance of God and in contempt of His rights and those of His Prophet. When my letter reaches you, go to them with your horses and men, and strike off their hands. If anyone defends them against you, or stands between them and you, expostulate with him, telling him the enormity of the sin and enmity which he is committing; and if he repents, accept his repentance, but if he declines, break off negotiations with him and proceed to hostilities — God will not guide the traitors! However, I think, nay I am sure, that no man will condone the evil acts of these women or hinder you from smiting them away from the religion of Muhammad as one might smite off the wings of a gnat.[20]

If we interpret this opposition between a group of women and Islam as a clash of interests, we have to analyze what interests were at stake. First we have to identify the parties. The identity of the first Caliph is indisputable, but that of the women is not. The Muslim document dismisses them summarily as harlots. But this ''harlotry'' was indeed an unusual one. The Muslim historian, Ibn Habib Al Bagdadi, identifies twelve of them. Two were grandmothers, one a mother, and seven were young girls. Three of the twelve belonged to the *ashraf* (''the noble class'') and four to the tribe of Kindah, a royal tribe which provided Yemen with its kings.[21] Some of the men who intervened to defend the women against the Muslim governor's forces were from this very royal tribe. What kind of harlotry is practiced by elderly grandmothers, young girls, by the most noble of women, the members of princely houses? And why, anyway, was the clapping of tambourines by twenty-six women in the faraway villages of South Arabia so threatening to the powerful military Muslim order?

A.F.L. Beetson explains the clash between the women and Islam as the clash between the old religion and the new.[22] He speculates that these women dissidents were deprived by the new religion of their position as pagan priest-esses of the old temples where religious prostitution was practiced. This speculation is not altogether warranted by the text.

The text, however, does make two things clear. First, some women opposed Islam because it jeopardized their position. Whatever that position was, it was evidently more advantageous than the one Islam granted them. Second, the opposition between these women and Islam clearly was in the sexual field. The fact that the Caliph labeled his opponents as harlots implies that Islam condemned their sexual practices, whatever they were, as harlotry. I believe that the Harlots of Hadramaut incident is an example of Islam's opposition to the sexual practices existing in pre-Islamic Arabia.

MATRILINEAL TRENDS IN PRE-MUSLIM SOCIETY

Robertson Smith pointed to the sixth and seventh centuries as a transitional phase in Arab kinship history. He characterized the period of Islam's appearance as having a multiplicity of sexual unions belonging to two trends: a matrilineal trend which he calls *sadica* marriage,[23] and a patrilineal trend he calls *ba'al* or dominion marriage.[24] The two systems, which existed side by side down to the Prophet's time,[25] were diametrically opposed to each other. Not only were they governed by different laws of kinship, but they "imply fundamental differences in the position of women and so in the whole structure of the social relations."[26] The difference between the two systems can be summarized as follows:

	Matrilineal Trend	*Patrilineal Trend*
Kinship rule	Child belonged to the mother's group	Child belonged to the father's group
Paternity rule	Physical paternity unimportant: the genitor does not have rights over his off-spring	Physical paternity important because the genitor must be the social father
Sexual freedom of the woman	Extended, her chastity has no social function	Limited, her chastity is a prerequisite for the establish-ment of the child's legitimacy
Status of the woman	Depends on her tribe for protection and food	Depends on her husband for protection and food
Geographical setting of marriage	Uxorilocal	Virilocal

Sadica marriage (from *sadic,* "friend," and *sadica,* "female friend") is a union whose offspring belong to the woman's tribe. It is initiated by a mutual agreement between a woman and a man and takes place at the house of the woman, who retains the right to dismiss the husband. In *ba'al* marriage the offspring belong to the husband. He has the status of a father as well as that of his wife's *ba'al,* i.e., "lord," "owner." In such a marriage:

The wife, who follows her husband and bears his children, who are of his blood, loses the right freely to dispose of her person. Her husband has authority over her and he alone has the right of divorce.[27]

Robertson Smith concludes that Islam speeded up the transition from matriliny to patriliny by enforcing a marriage institution which had very much in common with the patrilineal dominion marriage, and by condemning as *zina* all matrilineal unions:

> Certainly Mecca made no exception to the rule that Arabian *Ba'al* marriage was regarded as constituted by capture or by purchase, that the marital rights of the husband were a dominion over his wife, and that the disposal of her hand did not belong to the woman herself but to her guardian. For all this is still true even under Islam; the theory of Moslem law is still that marriage is purchase, and the party from whom the husband buys is the father, though by a humane illogicality the price becomes the property of the woman, and the husband's rights are not transferable. And so, though Islam softened some of the harshest features of the old law, it yet has set a permanent seal of subjection on the female sex by stereotyping a system of marriage which, at bottom, is nothing else than the old marriage of dominion.[28]

Sadica marriage was characterized by the woman's sexual freedom, symbolized by her sovereignty over the marital household, i.e., the tent in which she receives her husband:

> The women in Jahiliya, or some of them, had the right to dismiss their husbands, and the form of dismissal was this: if they lived in a tent, they turned it around so that if the door faced East, it now faced West, and when the man saw this, he knew that he was dismissed, and he did not enter.[29]

It is evident that this kind of marriage could not but be uxorilocal since the woman remained with her tribe and depended on it. The symbolic gesture of dismissal was known as ''she draws a curtain between the husband and herself'' and was used in the case of Muhammad Ibn Bachir whose wife ''drew a curtain between him and her and disappeared.''[30]

The variety of sexual unions practiced in pre-Islamic Arabia is best described by the trustworthy Muslim traditionist, Bukhari:

> Ibn Shihab said, Urwah B. Az Zubair informed him that Aicha, the wife of the Prophet (God bless and perserve him) informed him that marriage in the Jahiliyah was of four types:
>
> 1 — *One was marriage of people as it is today* where a man betroths his ward or his daughter to another man, and the latter assigns a dowry [bride wealth] to her and then marries her.
>
> 2 — *Another type was where a man said to his wife when she was purified from her menses, send to N. and ask to have intercourse with him;* her husband then stays away from her and does not touch her at all until it is clear that she is pregnant from that [other] man with whom she sought intercourse. When it is clear that she is

pregnant, her husband has intercourse with her if he wants. He acts thus simply from the desire for a child. This type of marriage was known as Nikah Al Istibda [''the marriage of seeking intercourse''].

3 — *Another type was where a group of less than ten men used to visit the same woman* and all of them to have intercourse with her. If she became pregnant and bore a child, when some nights had passed after the birth she could send for them, and not a man of them might refuse. When they had come together in her presence, she would say to them, ''You [plural] know the result of your acts. I have borne a child and he is your [singular] child, N.'' naming whoever she will by his name; her child is attached to him and the man may not refuse.

4 — *The fourth type is where many men frequent a woman,* and she does not keep herself from any who comes to her. These women are the *baghaya* [prostitutes]. They used to set up at their doors banners forming a sign. Whoever wanted them, went in to them. If one of them conceived and bore a child, they gathered together to her and summoned the physiognomists to designate as father the man whom the child resembled most. Then the child remained attached to him and was called his son, no objection to this course being possible. When Muhammad (God bless and perserve him) came preaching the truth, he destroyed all the types of marriage of the Jahiliyah except that which people practice today. [numbers mine].[31]

The general picture which emerges from Bukhari's description is a system characterized by the coexistence of a variety of marriages, or rather sexual unions. In three of the four kinds of marriages, physical paternity seems unimportant and therefore the concept of female chastity is absent (2, 3, and 4). Two of the marriages were polyandrous, the woman having as many 'husbands' as she desired (3 and 4).

Another kind of marriage mentioned elsewhere by Bukhari is *Mut'a* (''marriage of pleasure, or temporary marriage''):

> If a man and a woman agree to live together, their partnership lasts three nights and if they want to extend it, they extend it, and if they decide to part, they part.[32]

Tarmidi gives a description of the practicality of such a union:

> In early Islam, when the man used to arrive in a new town where he did not know anybody, he married a woman in exchange for a sum of money according to the length of the period of his stay, and she kept his belongings and took care of him. This was practiced until the verse forbidding it was revealed.[33]

Its sexual goal is affirmed in another traditionist's description. Imam Muslim writes:

> *Mut'a* . . . was a temporary marriage. The man will say to the woman, ''I will enjoy you for a certain period of time in exchange for a certain sum of money.'' It was named *Mut'a* [pleasure] because its main purpose was exclusively sexual pleasure, i.e., without procreation and other purposes usually expected from marriage. *Mut'a* was outlawed by the Book and the Sunna.[34]

It was practiced in early Islam and is still practiced by Muslims who follow the *Shia* trend.[35]

Compared to orthodox Muslim marriage, *Mut'a* violates two fundamental principles of Islam's ideal of sexual union:

1. Its temporary and personal character gives the woman as much freedom as the man, in both the initiation and the termination of the marriage. Muslim marriage reserves these rights to the man only, subordinates the woman's consent to that of her guardian, and alienates her freedom to divorce by subordinating it to a judge's decision.
2. Such a union implies different paternity rules than the ones on which Muslim marriage is based, i.e., the rule according to which the social father must be the physical genitor. For Robertson Smith:

> *Mut'a* in short is simply the last remains of that type of marriage which corresponds to a law of mother-kinship, and Islam condemns it and makes it 'the sister of harlotry' because it does not give the husband a legitimate offspring, i.e., an offspring that is reckoned to his own tribe and has right of inheritance within it.[36]

The panorama of female sexual rights in pre-Islamic culture reveals that women's sexuality was not bound by the concept of legitimacy. Chidren belonged to their mother's tribe. Women had sexual freedom to enter into and break off unions with more than one man, either simultaneously or successively. The woman could either reserve herself to one man at a time, on a more or less temporary basis, as in a *mut'a* marriage, or she could be visited by many husbands at different times whenever their nomadic tribe or trade caravan came through the woman's town or camping ground.[37] The husband would come and go; the main unit was the mother and child within an entourage of kinfolk.[38]

The linguistic legacy of the matrilineal past has survived to our day in Arabic. The word *rahim*, meaning the "womb," is "the most general word for kinship."[39] *Batn*, ("belly") is the technical term for a clan or a sub-tribe.[40] The word *umm* ("mother") is the origin of Umma ("community" in general and, after Islam, the Muslim community). According to Salama Musa, the fact that the word *haya*, which means life, is also a name for the reproductive apparatus of the woman, expresses the old Arab belief which endowed the woman with the gift of giving life and limited the male's role to "pure sexual pleasure."[41]

Robertson Smith copiously documents the shift from patrilineal to matrilineal marriage with examples from both Muslim and pre-Islamic sources.[42]

THE EFFECTS OF MUSLIM MARRIAGE ON PRE-MUSLIM SOCIETY

If we consider marriage as a "rearrangement of social structure" and social structure as "any arrangement of persons in institutionalized relationships,"[43] then a change in the marriage system would imply far reaching socio-economic changes. A change in kinship implies a dislocation of old socio-economic structures, and the appearance of new socio-economic networks based on new units. In *Muhammad at Mecca* and *Muhammad at Medina,*[44] Montgomery Watt analyzes Arabia's socio-economic foundations in the transitional period during the sixth and early seventh centuries. He traces Islam's sweeping success among the tribes (Muhammad started preaching in 613, and when he died in 632 most of Arabia's tribes were already converted) to a pre-existing malaise caused by the disintegration of the tribal system. Insecurities and discontent were spreading because of the rise of a thriving mercantile economy which was corroding the traditional tribal communalism. Individuals engaged in trading were motivated by new mercantile allegiances which often clashed with traditional tribal allegiances.[45] In thriving urban settlements like Mecca, the contradictions between new and old allegiances were particularly acute. The violation of traditional allegiances brought about isolation and economic insecurity among the weakest members of the tribe. Responsible members of the tribe who were supposed to administer property for the communal good were now lured by individualistic pursuits and neglected their traditional role as protectors of the weak.[46] Women and children were among those most directly affected by the disruption of the old networks of solidarity since they had no institutionalized access to property through inheritance.[47] Inheritance was the privilege of those who took part in battles and acquired booty, i.e., able-bodied adult males.

But if women did not have the right to inherit, it does not mean that they had no access to goods, as some Muslim writers believe.[48] Their protection and economic well-being was the core of a tribe's prestige and the embodiment of its honor.[49] It has been argued that many of Islam's institutions were a response to the new needs which emerged with the disintegration of tribal communalism, a means of absorbing the insecurities generated by such a disintegration. Polygamy, for example, has been explained as such an institution.[50] The Prophet, concerned about the fate of women who were divorced, widowed or unmarried orphans, decided to create a kind of responsibility system whereby unattached women were resituated in a family unit where a man could protect them, not just as a kinsman, but as a husband. The fact that polygamy was instituted by the Quran after the Disaster of Uhud where many Muslim males were slain, substantiates this theory.[51]

Moreover, the Prophet had a vested interest in having women, made helpless by the breakdown of tribal solidarity, reintegrated into new solidarity units, because otherwise they were likely to seek protection in transitory sexual unions considered as *zina* by Islam. It is here that one sees the genius of Islam. The appropriateness of its institutions is shown by its success in connecting both communal and self-serving tendencies and channeling these otherwise contradictory trends into the most cohesive social order Arabia has ever known. The communal tendencies were channeled into warfare for the *Pax Islamica*, and the self-serving tendencies were mainly given release in the institution of the family which allowed new allegiances, new ways to transfer private possession of goods, while providing at the same time tight controls over women's sexual freedom.

Watt suggests that the *Umma* resembled the tribe in many of its premises. The responsibility system within the *Umma* was very similar to the tribal principles of blood-feud and the *lex talionis:*

> For the military prestige of the *Umma*, it was essential in Arabian conditions that a Muslim should never go unavenged.[52]

But the *Umma* steered the tribes' bellicosity, usually invested in tribal feuding, in a new direction — the holy war.[53] The old allegiance to the tribe was replaced by an allegiance entirely different in both form and content. The form is the *Umma,* and the basic unit is not the tribe, but the individual.[54] The tie is not kinship but a more abstract concept, communion in the same religious belief.

In less than a few decades, the *Razzia*-inclined nomadic tribes, which were a great obstacle to Arabia's thriving trade routes and centers, were persuaded to give in to the *Umma*, which required unconditional surrender to the will of Allah. Consequently, their quest for booty was deflected from internal attacks and channeled into the holy war against the common enemy. The wealthy Byzantine and Persian Empires fell to the Arabs before they were fully aware of the existence of Islam. (Persia was conquered in 642, twenty years after the Hijra. The first siege of Constantinople took place in 670.)

Parallel to the harnessing of tribal bellicosity in the service of the Muslim community, there was a similar absorption of self-serving tendencies into the family structure. One of these channeling mechanisms was the concept of fatherhood and legitimacy, which allowed full expression to the believers' self-interest.

It would be natural for him [any man in an increasingly patrilineal society] at the same time to become specially interested in his own children and to want them to succeed to the wealth he had appropriated. In a matrilineal family, the control of the family property would normally pass from a man to his sister's son.[55]

For a man to transfer his goods to his sons implies that he has sons, which had not generally been clear. Physical paternity had been considered unimportant in the pre-existing systems, and the patterns of female sexuality made it rather difficult to establish who begot whom. Islam dealt with this obstacle in two ways. As we have seen, it outlawed most previous sexual practices as *zina* and institutionalized a strict control over paternity in the form of the *idda*, or waiting period. The *idda* can be seen both as the best proof of the previous disregard for physical paternity and as the best proof of the Islamic curtailment of female sexual rights, since no equivalent period was instituted for men.

The obsession to eradicate the woman's power to decide paternity is, as the institution of the *idda* shows, rather difficult to realize without the cooperation of the woman. The *idda* implies that the Muslim God does not expect the woman's cooperation although he explicitly requires it as a condition of the woman's oath of allegiance. Verse 228 of Surah II declares,

It is not lawful for them [women] that they should conceal that which Allah hath created in their wombs, if they are believers in Allah . . .

The fact that Allah, despite his unequivocal orders to the woman, decided to check on her by institutionalizing the waiting period shows that he did not expect her to obey the divine order. The expectation that the woman will not cooperate, that she will need to be coerced, explains the man's religious duty to control the women under his roof. The man is responsible not only to satisfy the woman sexually and provide for her economically, but, as a policeman of the Muslim order, he is also responsible to discipline and guard his female relatives.

Watt noticed that the idea of a police force distinct from the community was unknown among the Arabs.[56] A rigid code of honor compelled every individual to suit his actions, which were entirely involved in communal pursuit, to the community's standards. In Islam, the same mechanism operated but the man's burden was heavier because the *Umma* conceded him an individual territory of which he would be the master and for which he would be held responsible: "The man is the guardian of his family and he is responsible . . ."[57]

The social order created by the Prophet, a patrilineal monotheistic state, could only exist if the tribe and its allegiances gave way to the *Umma*. The Prophet found the institution of the family a much more suitable unit for socialization than the tribe. He saw the tightly controlled patriarchal family as necessary to the creation of the *Umma*.

The Prophet's religious vision, his personal experiences and the structure of the society he was reacting against, all contributed to the form Islamic society took. The assumptions behind the Muslim social structure — male dominance, the fear of *fitna,* the need for sexual satisfaction, the need for men to love Allah above all else — were embodied in specific laws which have regulated male-female relations in Muslim countries to this day.

But modernization is disrupting the traditional patterns of male-female interactions. Since modernization grants women more independence and self-determination, modern Muslim society is in some ways moving closer to pre-Muslim sexual patterns. Part II will explore the changes occurring because of modernization, and the consequent disruptions of the society, both within and without the family. Any change in male-female relations is a threat to the Umma's strength and a direct attack on the traditional coherence between Muslim ideology and Muslim reality.

PART II

*Anomic Effects of Modernization
on Male-Female Dynamics*

CHAPTER 4

The Modern Situation:
A Description of The Data

I have outlined a theoretical model of the traditional Muslim concept of female sexuality based on Ghazali's ideas of Muslim marriage. I want to use his description of the Muslim family not to evaluate the historical changes in that family, but to better understand the present situation by contrasting it with an ideal type. I will compare Ghazali's ideal family with the Moroccan reality as revealed by the data I have collected, in order to illustrate the trends shaping modern male-female dynamics.

I collected my data in Morocco in the summer of 1971. At first my main concern was how to investigate the changes occurring in male-female dynamics. I casually asked about fifty people (roughly half males and half females), ''What do you think is the main change which has taken place in the family and the woman's situation in the last decades?''

Almost everyone I interviewed mentioned, at one point or another, sexual desegregation. The idea was presented in different ways, such as, ''before women were protected,'' ''before women were not everywhere,'' ''before women were sitting in their homes,'' or ''before there was more order; women were strictly controlled,'' but the underlying idea was always the same. So I decided to concentrate on the dimension of male-female dynamics where the changes seem to have been particularly noticeable — the use of space by the sexes.

I wanted to get two kinds of data if possible: data describing family life in both traditional and modern settings (where the wife holds a job outside the home or has free access to the outside world) and data describing the present tensions in Moroccan society relating to sexual interaction. I opted for lengthy interviews with women to get the first kind of data. For the second, I used letters from the Radiodiffusion Television Marocaine's religious counselling service which daily receives hundreds of letters from citizens with problems. I was allowed to borrow 402 of these letters.

THE INTERVIEW WITH WOMEN

Because of the theoretical nature of my research and the extent of what I wanted to investigate — sexual desegregation — I decided to limit my scope as much as possible. I selected data concerning one numerically tiny strata of the Moroccan population — the urban petite bourgeoisie. Despite its size it has played an important political role in other Arabo-Muslim societies and is likely to do the same in the Moroccan future.

The interviews were held in the summer of 1971 with fourteen women: eight traditional women and six modern ones. The classification traditional/modern covers a whole range of differences like age, education and type of employment. See Figure 1 (see page 49) for a description of the contrasts between the traditional women and the modern ones.

Figure 2 (see page 49) lists the age and marital status of each of the women I interviewed. It also gives the occupation of each modern woman and the occupation of the man supporting each traditional woman.

In order to examine more closely the trends of modernization I tried to interview mothers (traditional) with their daughters (modern). I succeeded only four times in realizing this combination. They are indicated in the chart by the same last initial.

The interviews were non-directed, lengthy, in-depth interviews run on the normal rhythm of a "gossip" exchange. Very often the interviews were recorded in more than one session depending on the mood, the interruptions, etc.

I concentrated on just a few interviews as sources for quotation in order to increase the reader's familiarity with the individuals described. Within a section, I used information from one interview as much as possible. For example, the interviewee coded Fatiha F. was used as the main source for the section on the mother-in-law not only because Fatiha is a wonderful conversationalist, but also because the contradictions of the relation mother-son-wife reaches an almost archetypal dimension in her case.

A systematic reading of (or rather listening to) the tapes of the interviews revealed two major differences between the lives of traditional women and those of modern women. For the traditional women sexual segregation had been very strict all their lives. For the modern women sexual segregation had been strict only during puberty when they were made aware of the importance of their behavior to the family honor. The modern women did not feel that sexual segregation was an important factor in their lives now.

The other major difference between the traditional and the modern women was their perception of who was the most important person in their daily lives, what person they had the most intense relationship with. For the traditional women it was their mother-in-law. For the modern women it was their husband. That these are the major differences suggests a link between the institution of sexual segregation and the important role in the family traditionally accorded to the husband's mother. But I had no clue as to the nature of the link until I had done a content analysis of the letters to the radio station.

THE COUNSELLING LETTERS

The 400 letters analysed are a sample of the thousands of letters sent to a counselling service financed and run by the government. It is broadcast daily on The national network which has, besides entertainment programs, many community-oriented projects. For example, divorces pronounced by the judge on the grounds of desertion are announced on the radio thereby disseminating information to a large number of illiterate Moroccans who would otherwise not have access to this information. The counselling service is another community-oriented service undertaken by the national network.

Counselling has always been an important procedure in Moslem life because of the freedom accorded to the individual. There is no clergy, no institutionalized intermediary between the individual and God. Every sensible adult is responsible for his thoughts and deeds. To be a decent believer one needs, more than anything else, the intention to be so — that is, the intention to subordinate one's acts to the divine law. Whenever the individual doubts his knowledge of divine law he is to seek guidance from people trained in the matter. The Cadi Moulay Mustapha Alaoui, whose services are free of charge and delivered by radio, is probably the most popular counsellor in the country. He usually gathers letters by subject and tries to answer one specific theme each day. It is the themes emerging in the letters which dictated their codification and content analysis.

Thanks to the Arabic formula which heads most letters ''From Mr. or Mrs. so and so, from the town of so and so'' the sex and origin of the letter-writers were usually identifiable. The letters also frequently mention the age and marital status of the letter-writer. An analysis of the sex, geographical distribution, marital status and age of the letter-writers appears in Figure 3 (see page 50). Whenever the handwriting was too difficult to decipher or the information was lacking, the letter was coded blank.

The coding for the content analysis was suggested by the themes which emerged from reading the letters. The majority of letters dealt with problems relating to the family. The way I coded the content of the letters is illustrated by some examples of the variables I found under the heading, Pre-Marital Tensions.

Variable (9) The youth's decision to marry
    1—Falling in love
    2—Wanting to marry the person of one's own choice
    3—Combination of 1 and 2

Variable (10) The parents' stand
    1—Parents interfere in offspring's choice
    2—Parents oppose overtly the offspring's choice
    3—Parents force the offspring to marry a person of the parents' choice
    4—Combination of 1 and 2
    5—Combination of 1 and 3

Variable (14) Parents' response to children's marital plans
    1—Curse
    2—Threaten to curse
    3—Open conflict son-family
    4—Open conflict daughter-family

As is evident from the kinds of themes I found, a controversial question in modern Morocco is who chooses the marital partner? Is it the youth or the parents? According to the letters, parents think it their right to choose their offspring's partner in marriage, and the offspring think it their right to choose for themselves. The traditional Muslim ideas about marriage are in direct conflict with the ideas engendered in young people by modernization.

My data suggests, and I believe, that Islam's concepts of female sexuality and the woman's contribution to society (as I sketched them in Part I) still determine the primary features of the Muslim family. The role played by sexual segregation, arranged marriage, the mother's importance in her son's life, all seem to be part of a system which discourages heterosexual involvement even within the conjugal unit.

Modernization on the other hand encourages desegregation, independent choice of marriage partner and the mobility of the nuclear family. That this open clash of ideologies leads to confusion and anxiety is apparent both in the counselling letters and in the interviews with women.

I have tried to analyse the data I collected and make it intelligible. Consequently I hope I have rendered the behavior under study — male-female dynamics in modern Morocco — more intelligible. My pride as a social scientist lies not so much in my model being infallible, as in its being discussed, attacked, checked and revised. If I can stir thinking on the matter I will have achieved my goal.

Figures

Figure 1	*Traditional Women*	*Modern Women*
Literacy	Illiterate	Literate
Job	Work within the home	Work outside the home
Sexual Segregation	Very strict	Very loose
Marriage	Arranged by the parents	Woman chose own partner
Age	Born before World War II	Born after World War II (when the nationalists' influence opened up the schools for girls)

Figure 2

Traditional Women

	Marital Status	*Age*	*Occupation of the Male Supporting Her*
H-lima H.	Widowed	60	Son — Civil Servant
Hayat H.	Married	40	Husband — Civil Servant
Fatiha F.	Married	45	Husband — Civil Servant
Kenza	Married	50	Husband — Retired Civil Servant
Tamou T.	Widowed	48	Brother — Teacher
Khata	Married	48	Husband — Works in electric company
Salama	Widowed	60	Son — Agricultural Technician
Maria M.	Repudiated	55	Son — Army Officer

Modern Women

	Marital Status	*Age*	*Her Occupation*
Faiza F.	Married	22	Laboratory Assistant
Mona M.	Married	26	Teacher
Tahna T.	Single	25	Medical Student (works part-time and has grant)
Tama	Repudiated	30	Public Relations Officer
Lamia	Repudiated	30	Accountant
Safia	Single	25	Secretary

Figure 3

IDENTITY VARIABLES
SEX
(indicated in 369 letters)

	Number	Percentage
Female Writers	160	43
Male Writers	209	57

GEOGRAPHICAL ORIGIN OF THE LETTER
(indicated in 298 letters)

	Number	Percentage
Writers from Big Cities	210	70%
Writers from Elsewhere	88	30%

MARITAL STATUS
(indicated in 175 letters)

Singles	46%
Widowed	4%
Married	48%
Marriage Broken (Unspecified)	2%

AGE
(indicated in 107 letters)

Teenagers (Under 20)	45%
Young Adults (Between 20 and 25)	39%
Adults (Over 25)	8%
Elderly (When the writer describes himself thus)	8%

CHAPTER 5

Sexual Anomie As Revealed By The Data

Relations between the sexes seem to be going through a period of anomie, of deep confusion and absence of norms. The traditional norms governing relations between the sexes are violated every day by a growing majority of people without incurring legal or social sanctions. One such traditional norm is sexual segregation, the systematic prevention of interaction between men and women not related to each other either by marriage or by blood. Sexual segregation divides all social space into male spaces and female spaces.

The overlap between male and female areas is limited and regulated by a host of rituals. When a man invites a friend to share a meal at his house, he knocks on his own door and asks with a loud voice for the women "to make the way" (*'amlu triq*). The women then run to hide in dark corners, leaving the courtyard free to be crossed by the stranger. The guest will remain with his host, seated in the men's room, until he leaves. If he needs to go to the toilet, the ritual of *'amlu triq* is again staged, preventing the taboo situation of interaction between strangers of different sexes.

Similar rituals surround the trespassing of the woman into male spaces which was, until recently, limited to a very few occasions, — the visit to the Saint's tomb, the visit to the Hammam and the visits of relatives at births, deaths and marriages. The veil is an expression of the invisibility of women on the street, a male space par excellence.

According to my interviews, sexual segregation was lived as a natural part of life by women in their fifties, but it is merely an option for women now in their thirties. The woman's right to traditionally male spaces is far from being institutionalized or even accepted, whether at the level of the laws or of the underlying ideology. The anomie stems from the gap between the ideology and the reality, which is that more and more women are using traditionally male spaces, are going without the veil, and are deciding their own lives. The anomie created by the gap between ideology, belief and practice is well illustrated in the following letter received by the religious counselling service:

Casablanca, 18-5-1971   Letter 88
                    To his highness, professor Moulay Mustapha Alaoui
    Sir,
        Nowadays, the majority of the people go to swim in the sea, they go to beaches

during the summer months. Then, men, women, boys, and girls meet and mix together. They also mix with Christians and Jews; everyone looking at everybody else's nudity. Is this a permissible event in a Moslem society? I asked this question a long time ago. I did not hear your answer on the radio. Could it be that you did not recieve it?

Desegregation intensifies the sexual component of heterosexual interactions while the society fails to provide any acceptable models for sexual interactions. Doubts and anxieties generated by this situation are evident in the following letters.

Taza, 13-3-1971   Letter 46
                                    To the religious scholar Moulay Mustapha
Sir,
    I was in love with a young man. He asked me to allow him to kiss me and caress me. I gave in to his demands. I was encouraged in doing so by a girlfriend but we did not go as far as having intercourse. After a while I discovered that he was not serious about our relation and I kept away from him. And I promised myself that I would never commit such sinful practices again. Is what I have done permissible or forbidden by Islam? What can I do to erase such sin? Thank you! Thank you!

* * * * *

Rabat, 14-6-1971   Letter 100
                                    From Miss K . . . . . to his highness Pr. M. M.
I send you a perfumed salutation,
    Is it permissible for a young unmarried girl who is not engaged to be kissed by a man who is not engaged to her and does not intend to marry her? I will be very thankful if you can answer my question with as many details as you can. Many thanks, sir.

A content analysis of the 402 letters reveals that sexuality (presented in terms of questions about love, marriage, deviant practices, etc.) seems to be one of the preoccupations of the letter-writers. The majority of the letters enquire about the permissibility or non-permissibility of sexual actions from the religious point of view. Most of the questions are about acts, like swimming "nude" (a woman is "nude" if she is not veiled) on a mixed-sex beach or being kissed by someone other than the legal husband, that are illicit and sinful according to tradition. The increased interaction between the sexes is still an unusual phenomenon in Moroccan society. The traditional, absolute segregation between the sexes continues to pervade many parts of the country.

SEXUAL PROBLEMS IN RURAL AREAS: HETEROSEXUAL RELATIONS OUTLAWED

A survey of some rural areas[1] revealed that each village controls its youth to such an extent that young men have no access to women and engage in deviant sexual practices, by the society's own standards. For example, of those who answered the questionnaire,

14%—confessed practicing masturbation or sodomy

20%—practice homosexuality

34%—go to a brothel in the nearest town as often as they can afford it.[2]

There are no thorough studies of the sexual practices of Moroccan youth in general, so we can draw no firm conclusions about sexual problems in general.

Almost two-thirds of Morocco's fifteen million people live in rural areas,[3] and fifty-six percent of the total population are under the age of twenty.[4] In the rural areas surveyed, 87 percent of the people were under the age of twenty-one, and 78 percent of these youths dreamed of going to live in town. One of the reasons they gave for that preference was that in towns women are available.

> In town there are as many girls as you want.
> You can find brothels only in towns.
> In town women walk with heads uncovered, wearing short dresses; you can always take a chance with them.[5]

Sexual segregation is enforced in one village with a characteristically violent censure:

> If you try to leave the village with a girl who is more than twelve years old, more than thirty people will follow you. They start throwing stones and shouting at you. It is not like in town; you need to take so many measures.[6]

The rural Moroccan male is brought, because of the restrictions on heterosexual encounters, to perceive the woman solely in terms of sexual need; both in and outside of marriage the woman is merely a more suitable way to satisfy sexual needs than animals or other males.

> At the age of seventeen I became aware of what was going on. I left animals and friends [with whom he practiced homosexuality] because I realized it was detrimental to my energy. I learned that one can find whores in the center of B_____. When I don't have money I don't hesitate to steal something so that I can go about my business.[7]

Most of the young men are resentful of being forced into sexual practices they abhor. They dream of getting married, and do so as soon as they can find a job, which is rather difficult. Unemployment, which takes the form of under-employment in the countryside, often reaches a huge percentage.[9] According to the 1971 census, those suffering most from uneployment are from fifteen to twenty-four years old. When looking for a job for the first time 83 percent of this group cannot find one.[10] The young men resent the fact that older men who ha've more money monopolize and marry most of the young girls.

> I fell in love with a girl in the village and she was aware of it. I did not have money . . . A civil servant [a man who has a job and who is from a more important urban center] came along and took away the girl I loved. So, I will not hide this from you, I went back to animals again.[11]

In the most traditional rural society, there are no unmarried adolescent girls. A survey done among the female rural population by Malika Belghiti, reveals that 50 percent of the girls are married before they reach puberty, and 37 percent more marry during the first two years following puberty.[12] One way the rural society avoids the problem of sexual love between young people seems to be the early marriage of girls.

The ideal age for marriage in the traditional structure according to my interviews with traditional women is thirteen. Early marriage is conceived of as a prestigious event in a woman's life. It implies that she was beautiful enough to be asked for early. Only ugly, unattractive girls marry late. Without exception, all of the women interviewed said they married before having their first period and gave the age of thirteen, when they were asked to give a specific age. I had the chance to check on one of them: I asked a childhood friend of hers if she remembered when Mrs. F_____ got married:

> She lied to you! She was a very old girl when she got married. She was a problem for her family. Have not you noticed that she was rather homely?
> (How old do you think she was when she got married?)
> I swear she must have been at least twenty! I wish I was there when you were interviewing her. She would not have dared to indulge herself. And how could you believe it? No one will call her a beauty, and don't tell me it is old age! She always was as ugly as famine days.

In urban Morocco girls seem to marry much later. A family planning survey by the government in 1966[13] revealed that the ideal age of marriage for girls in towns is much later than puberty:

Ideal Age at Marriage	For Men	For Women
According to Men	23	17
According to Women	25	19

Young men in towns have a chance to seek adolescent women of their own age and think about marrying them, while in rural settings all the young girls belong to husbands already.

SEXUAL PROBLEMS IN URBAN AREAS: HETEROSEXUAL LOVE THWARTED

Our data deals mainly with urban problems; 70 percent of the letters come from urban centers. They convey the ideal that sexual segregation in the city is not as absolute as it is in rural areas: young men actually do have access to women, often older women and/or married women.

Casablance, 1971   Letter 89

I am a fifteen year old high school student. Please guide me. Here is my problem: there is a married maid in our house. She cannot bear children; she is sterile. I used to be with her often and I used to visit her in her house and then I started sleeping with her. I mean, to commit *zina* with her. I did this many times. Please guide me. What can I do to redeem myself?

* * * * *

Casablance, 1-16-1971   Letter 169

I am a twenty-year-old man. I am trapped by a problem that I cannot solve. In our neighborhood lives a thirty-five-year-old woman who has children but no husband. I made advances to her once and what was bound to happen happened. I am asking God for forgiveness. After that I kept away from her. Two years have passed since then and now I look at her differently, as if she was my mother or my sister. In fact, our relation has evolved into a respectful, brotherly relation.

Now I am coming to the subject. This woman has a seventeen-year-old daughter who used to live with her grandmother and who has just come to stay with her mother. At the beginning I never gave her much attention, but I always noticed her kind manner towards me. I also noticed that she was very affectionate towards me. One day she confessed to me that she was in love with me and I responded to her affections . . .

But I can't forget what happened between her mother and me and often I am torn between my love for her and the desire to flee from her. She is an ideal girl for me and I feel a lot of affection for her. Once, she extracted from me the promise to marry her.[14] Moreover, my mother suggested her as a possible bride for me. I am trapped. There is no reason I should refuse. IS THIS MARRIAGE POSSIBLE, IS IT LICIT ACCORDING TO THE RELIGIOUS LAW?[15]

But most of the letters reveal that young men in towns seek contact with girls of the same age, want to marry them, and when they succeed in getting engaged, go further than a kiss.

Casablance, 17-5-1971   Letter 180

Sir,

I am twenty-three years old. I met a girl who is nineteen years old. I fell in love with her and went to her parents and asked her hand in marriage. We have had to wait for a while before getting married because I don't have enough money for that yet.

But, one day our sexual desire overwhelmed us and, therefore, I deprived her of her "treasure," of her "honor." This happened after we had written the marriage contract though. We don't want to tell her parents because we have not had the marriage ceremony yet. Does the religious law forbid what we did? My bride is as anxious as I because she has to live with her parents until the ceremony can take place.

But all young men are not as lucky as the above. The desire to marry girls of their own choosing brings strong opposition from the parents. Consequently, sexuality in urban centers often assumes the aspect of a generational conflict between parents and children. Twenty percent of the 402 letters center around this conflict. They reveal the young people's inclinations, their parents' attitudes and often how the conflict is resolved. An examination (i.e., cross-tabulation) of these themes and other variables such as age, sex, size of the town, gives an interesting insight into the shape of the conflict.

PARENTAL OPPOSITION TO LOVE MARRIAGE

The conflict centers around the parent's customary right to arrange marriage, and the young people's rejection of this right and insistence upon their right to love-marriage. The parents believe the choice of a sexual partner for their daughter or son is their decision. (Incidentally, this gives them tremendous power over their children's lives.) Young Moroccans claim that they should choose their own sexual partners. The younger the individual, the more likely he is to insist on his right to love as he chooses. Of the letters concerning this conflict, 70 percent are written by teenagers and 30 percent by individuals between twenty and twenty five. (we will call this category young adults).

Agadir, June 1971   Letter 5
                              From Mr. _____

I am a twenty-two-year-old man. I have a father; I lost my mother when I was a child. My father got married after my mother's death. I asked my maternal aunt's daughter to marry me in 1961. (Children's engagements have disappeared in general but if there is a strong attraction between young people it is common for the young man to make it known so that no one can take his beloved cousin from him). My father opposed this marriage knowing how much I loved this girl. This year I decided to marry her during the summer holidays. My father has announced that he will not be present at my marriage and that he will do whatever he can to prevent this marriage from taking place. He wants to force me to leave the girl I have loved for so many years in order to marry a girl of his choice whom I have never met but who happens to belong to my father's wife's family.

How can I solve such a problem? Can I marry the girl I love? What does the religious law say about a person of my age who marries without the father's approval? What does God say about this? My stepmother is the one who encourages my father to refuse my marriage.

* * * * *

Fez, 8-6-71 Letter 6

I am employed as a clerk in a company. I have a father who lives in the country far from me. I met a girl I want to marry and I promised to marry her and she promised to marry me. I wrote to my father announcing the news hoping that he will rejoice with me but he did not. He opposes the marriage. He wants me to marry a woman from the country. I cannot do that because I cannot conceive of my life without this girl anymore and if I try to part with her I might find myself in a situation which is dangerous not only for me but for the Muslim Umma as well, and for the Muslim religion too.

Please advise me about what is best for us and our religion.

The love protest voiced by young men is echoed by young women. The most fanatical advocates of the couple's rights, they write 70 percent of the letters about love.

Letter 7

From Miss ———

I am fifteen years old. A man came and asked for my hand from my parents. He has a bad temper and bad manners. He likes forbidden things like smoking, but kif. [Smoking kif, despite what Western tourists think, is considered a shameful addiction.] And of course my parents gave me to him. I have not accepted the marriage and I am not going to. But the problem is that when the contract is about to be written by the justice officer [Remember, it's a guardian who gives the girl in marriage], they do not intend to let me know. They intend to take another girl and write a fake contract. Then I will be sacrificed. My last decision if they write the contract is definite: I will commit suicide to free myself from this oppressive people. What does the religious law say concerning parents who fake their daughter's marriage? I prefer to kill myself whatever the law says.

Nonetheless, while 80 percent of the boys express their intention to marry their beloved, only 20 percent of the girls dare to go as far as that. This is probably due to the fact that, although "modern," Moroccan girls, like their grandmothers, think it is the man who should ask for the girl's hand and not the other way around. This attitude seems to be wise and realistic given the fact that according to the Moroccan law a woman cannot marry herself, a male guardian has to give her in marriage.

The fact that girls do not initiate marriage is probably also the reason why there is a very low percentage of conflicts between parents and daughters as compared with the conflicts between parents and sons. Of 14 cases where the conflict between parents and offspring had reached a crisis situation, ten concern the parents' opposition to the son's projected marriage.

The main weapon the parents use against the children seems to be the curse, the parents being invested with Allah's power to curse or bless their children.[16] The potential destructiveness of the parents' curse is dramatized by a traditional fear expressed in sayings and proverbs. One of the most common is:

Who is Cursed by parents cannot be saved by saints,
Who is cursed by saints can be saved by parents.

Persons cursed by their parents are likely to fail in whatever they try to do; their marriage will break up; their house will burn; their business enterprise will go bankrupt; in sum, a dreadful fate is to be expected on earth while waiting for hell in the next world. Consequently, parental opposition to children's marital projects is generally quite effective. Some young people say they feel resentment towards the unjust choice between their parents' blessings and their lover; some say they feel rebellious towards their parents but are afraid to act, they feel paralyzed; some plan to go ahead and act against their parents' will; and finally some threaten such drastic actions as breaking off relations with the parents or even committing suicide.

Why is Moroccan society, in the form of parental authority, reacting so negatively to the young people's desire for marriages based on love? Does conjugal love constitute an attack on Islam's attempts to integrate sexuality into the society by subordinating the woman to the authority of the husband and outlawing love between them?

One feature of the sexual patterns which emerged from both the findings on the rural population and from my own data on the urban population is that the heterosexual relationship is certainly the locus of change and conflict. The society seems to have a systematically negative attitude towards heterosexual love. In rural areas the young people are prevented from forming any heterosexual relationships at all. In urban areas they are prevented from forming any permanent heterosexual relationships based on love.

In rural Morocco the access of young men to young women is subject to strict and apparently efficient control. In urban centers, access seems to be much less restricted. Young people meet each other frequently enough to fall in love and want to get married. Does this mean that sexual segregation is breaking down in urban areas?

I believe that sexual segregation, one of the main pillars of Islam's social control over sexuality, is breaking down. And it appears to me that the breakdown of sexual segregation allows the emergence of what the Muslim order condemns as a deadly enemy of civilization — love between men and women in general, and between husband and wife in particular.

CHAPTER 6

Husband and Wife

The dynamics of shared spaces between the sexes can best be understood by analyzing the functioning of the conjugal unit — the only model of heterosexual relationships that Muslim Moroccan society gives to its children.

The ideal wife for the believer, according to Ghazali, is,

> Beautiful, non-temperamental, with black pupils, and long hair, big eyes, white skin, and in love with her husband, and looking at no one but him.[1]

Ghazali explains that Arabic has a word, *aruba,*[2] meaning a woman in love with her husband, who feels like making love with him. This is one of the words which describes the women promised to the believers in Paradise.[3] He adds that the Prophet said that a woman who loves and obeys her husband is a grace from Allah. Such a woman would indeed be a miracle, given the conflict structure within the conjugal unit based on a *rapport de force* where the most likely outcome is the woman's dislike of and rebellion against her husband.

MARRIAGE AS CONFLICT

All the women interviewed talked about the perceived *l'entente conjugale* as a magic phenomenon: it smoothes all obstacles.

> When there is an *entente* between husband and wife, all obstacles can be overcome. Big crises become easy to deal with. When there is no *entente,* everything becomes a crisis.
>
> Fatiha F.

> We never fought each other. He always treated me as a guest, with a lot of respect; he will do things before I express the need for them. For example, the day I decide to clean the house thoroughly I will try, on my own, to move the sofas and the wooden boards. He runs out to the street and hires a maid or two to help me. It is a gift of God when there is respect.
>
> Hayat H.

> He never thwarted my wishes. I did my best to never thwart his. He is still treating me with the same consideration. He never raises his voice with me. He respected me and I treated him like a king. Praise to God. I hope my daughters will have the same luck as I.
>
> Kenza

The perception of the husband's love and respect as a miracle probably stems from the fact that the woman cannot legally demand respect or love. This is illustrated in the listing of respective duties and rights in the 1957 Moroccan *Code*:

Art. 36 — *The Rights of the Husband Vis-à-Vis His Wife*
1. Fidelity
2. Obedience according to the accepted standards
3. Breastfeeding, if possible, of the children born from the marriage
4. The management of the household and its organization
5. Deference towards the mother and father and close relatives of the husband

Art. 35 — *The Rights of the Wife Towards Her Husband*
1. Financial support as stated by the law, such as food, clothing, medical care, and housing
2. In case of polygamy, the right to be treated equally with the other wives
3. The authorization to go and visit her parents and the right to receive them according to limit imposed by the accepted standards
4. Complete liberty to administer and dispose of her possessions with no control on the part of the husband, the latter has no power over his wife's possessions.

Note that the husband owes no moral duties to his wife. Moreover, apart from the rights of the wife listed in numbers 1 and 4 above, all other rights the wife is supposed to have are, in fact, either restrictions of her freedom (like item 3) or restrictions on her claim on her husband's person (polygamy in item 2). She cannot expect fidelity. What she expects to get from her husband are orders, and what she expects to give is obedience. The relation is a power relation. This is emphasized and justified by a social order which encourages the husband to command his wife and not to love her, as Ghazali describes:

Some souls let themselves sometimes be completely overtaken by passionate love [for a woman]. It is pure madness. It is to ignore completely why copulation was created. It is to sink to the level of beasts as far as domination and mastery of oneself go. Because a man passionately in love does not look for the mere desire to copulate which is already the ugliest of all desires[4] and of which one should be ashamed, but he goes as far as to believe that this appetite cannot be satisifed except with a specific object [a particular woman]. A beast satisfies its sexual appetite where it can while this type of man [the man in love] cannot satisfy his sexual appetite except with his beloved. Thus he accumulates disgrace after disgrace and slavery after slavery. He mobilizes reason in order for it to serve appetite while reason was created to command and to be obeyed.[5]

The religious duty of the husband to command his wife is enforced by numerous sayings and proverbs in Moroccan folklore, some of which are supposed to be direct quotations from the Prophet and his disciples.

Ask your wife's opinion, but follow your own.
Ask your wife's opinion, but do the opposite.
Don't ever follow your wife's suggestions.[6]

The duty of the man to command his wife is embodied in his right to correct her by physical beating. The Koran itself recommends such a measure, but only as a last resort. If his wife rebels, the husband is instructed to scold her and then to stop having sexual intercourse with her. Only if these measures fail should he beat her to make her obey.[7] The right of correction, which was thought likely to be used to excess by the husband, was restricted by the Prophet (who was very kind to his wives) to "decent" proportions:

> Do not beat your wives like one beats a slave and then copulate with them at the end of the night.[8]

The fear of mistreatment and of beating is one of the reasons why the girl and her family usually prefer marriage to a husband who lives in the same neighborhood.

In modern Morocco, the woman can bring suit against her husband for beating her. But she has no recourse against her husband if she cannot establish physical evidence of the mistreatment. Even so, the mistreatment must have reached a demonstrably unbearable stage for her to obtain a divorce. It is the judge who must estimate whether the mistreatment is bearable or not and decide whether or not to issue a divorce.[9] Judges are not reputed to favor women in Moroccan society, which means that the right to beat his wife is an almost unchecked privilege of the husband.

In traditional Moroccan society there is no openly admitted behavioral pattern for the wife to express her physical love towards her husband, while an openly admitted behavioral pattern for her rejection of him does exist: the *karh*. If the wife, after the first few days of marriage, does not like her husband, she is said to become *harjat karha*, or "hateful." There is a ritualized behavior by which she expresses it. It usually consists, according to my interviews, of a complete refusal to share space with him (she will leave the room whenever her husband steps in) and/or communicate with him verbally. When the wife is *karha*, it is considered a catastrophe by the respective families and by the individuals involved. The woman's rejection of her husband, in spite of the usually binding nature of marriage for the woman, often ends in the breaking of the marital bond. The experience of one woman who was married when she was thirteen reveals that the parents who arrange the marriage are, contrary to what one might think, very concerned about their daughter's fate when their plans fail. Women usually are remarried soon after the *karha* experience and often block it out of their memories, as is illustrated in the following interview:

— Zahra and Hamid are not from the same father.
— What do you mean? Who is Hamid's father then?

— My first husband.
— You promised me to tell the story of your life, and you forget something as important as that?
— I really forgot it. It is not important anyway. I don't like to talk about it.
— How long did it last?
— He was our neighbor. His wife died and my parents arranged the marriage. When he got in the *dahsousa*[10] [tent] I hated him. It lasted one year and a half. I spent most of the time in my parents' house. He did everything he could to make me love him, but when he tried to get near me, it used to aggravate things. When I got pregnant, that was it. I'd see him and I'd start shivering. We organized my running away. My father arranged for me to go and stay with an uncle who was living far away from the town. The judge got involved in the affair. My father started sending delegations of *shorfas* [people who think they are, and are believed to be, direct descendants of the Prophet] to my husband's family. Finally, my poor father decided to buy my freedom, and I was liberated!

Tamou T.

Imam Ghazali agrees that marriage is equivalent to slavery for the woman because it places her in a situation where she "has to obey him [her husband] without restrictions, except in cases where what he asks her to do constitutes a flagrant violation of Allah's orders."[11]

Why does Moroccan society encourage the husband to take the role of master instead of lover? Does love between man and wife threaten something vital in the Muslim order? We have seen that sexual satisfaction is considered necessary to the moral health of the believer. There is no tension between Islam and sexuality as long as that sexuality is expressed harmoniously and is not frustrated. What Islam views as negative and anti-social is the woman and her power to create *fitna*. Heterosexual involvement, real love, is the danger which must be overcome.

THE PREVENTION OF INTIMACY

The sexual act is considered polluting[12] and is surrounded by ceremonials and incantations whose goal is to create an emotional distance between the spouses and reduce their embrace to its most elementary function — that of a purely reproductive act. During the coital embrace, the male is actually embracing a woman, symbol of unreason, disorder, the anti-divine force of nature and disciple of the devil. From this comes the dread of erection which is experienced as a loss of control and referred to, according to Ghazali,[13] as darkness in verse 3 of *Surah* 113:

Say: I seek refuge in the lord of daybreak
From the evil of that which he created
From the evil of darkness when it is intense.

In an attempt to prevent a complete merging with the woman, the coital embrace is surrounded by a ceremony which grants Allah a substantial presence in the man's mind during coitus. The coital space is religiously oriented: the couple should have their heads turned away from Mecca. "They should not face the "holy shrine" in respect for it."[14] The symbolism of spatial orientation expresses the antagonism between Allah and the woman. Mecca is the direction of God. During intercourse, the man is reminded that he is not in Allah's territory, whence the necessity to invoke his presence:

> It is advisable for the husband to start by invoking God's name and reciting 'Say God is one' first of all and then reciting the *Takbir* "God is the greater" and the *Tahlil* "There is no other divinity but God" and then say, "In the name of God the very high and very powerful, make it a good posterity if you decide to make any come from my kidney."[15]

At the crucial moment of ejaculation when the physical and spiritual boundaries of the lover melt away in a total identification with the woman,[16] the Muslim lover is reminded that:

> It is suitable to pronounce without moving the lips, the following words: "Praise to God who created men from a drop of water." [17]

The conjugal unit presents an even graver danger than the ephemeral sexual embrace; erotic love has the potential to grow and thrive into something much more encompassing, much more total. It has the potential to evolve into an emotional bond giving a man the plenitude "only God is supposed to give:"

> The erotic relation seems to offer the unsurpassable peak of the fulfillment of the request for love in the direct fusion of the souls of one to the other . . . A principal ethic of religious brotherhood is radically and antagonistically opposed to all this. From the point of view of such an ethic, this inner earthly sensation of salvation by mature love competes in the sharpest possible way with the devotion of a supra-mundane God . . .[18]

The Muslim God requires from his subjects a total love; he requires all of his believer's capacity for emotional attachment:

> Yet of mankind are some who take unto themselves [objects of worship which they set as] rivals to Allah, loving them with a love like [that which is due] Allah [only] those who believe are stauncher in their love for Allah.[19]

or, again:

> Emotional attachment divides man's heart, and Allah hath not created man with two hearts within his body.[20]

The Muslim God is acknowledged to be a jealous God, and he is acknowledged to be particularly jealous of anything which might interfere in the believer's devotion to him.[21] The conjugal unit is a real danger and is consequently weakened by two legal devices: polygamy and repudiation. Both institutions are based on psychological premises which reveal a puzzling knowledge of the couple's psychology and its weaknesses.

Folk wisdom perceives polygamy as a means for man to make himself valuable, not by perfecting any quality within himself, but simply by creating a competitive situation between many females:

> Tamou is a treasure chest [Tamou is a woman's name] Aicha is the key to it [Aicha is another woman's name].[22]

Polygamy is in this sense a direct attempt to prevent emotional growth in the conjugal unit, and results in the impoverishement of the husband's and wife's investment in each other as lovers.

> The obvious consequence of polygamy is that the wife does not 'own her husband,' she shares him with one or more co-wives. What does this mean? For one thing, it must mean that the polygamous husband tends to have a less emotional investment in any single wife. He does not have 'all his eggs in one basket.' The meaning for the co-wives is less clear. I suspect that polygamy has a general 'lowering effect' on the emotional importance of the husband-wife bond and that this applies to the wife as well as to the husband, she also invests less in her husband and 'invests' more in other relationships.[24]

The meaning of polygamy for the co-wives is clarified by Salama, a sixty-year-old woman who lived as a concubine in a Moroccan harem from 1924-1950:

> I was happy to be raised to the status of his lover but I was afraid of all the dangers attached to it.[25]
>
> (What dangers?)
>
> Many, the most frightening is the *hjar*.[26]
>
> (Did he ever *hjar* any of you?)
>
> Yes, he did. Zahra. He only solicited her once and never talked to her after that. I was obsessed by Zahra's case. Everytime I went to his apartments, I lay there wide awake in the dawn asking myself, 'Is it the last time he is to call me?' I was no different from Zahra. Zahra was more beautiful than many of us. Why will he choose me again?
>
> (Were you jealous?)
>
> You are funny. Jealous of whom? And of what? We had no rights. No one had any rights over him, including the legitimate wife. For once we were all equal, democracy.

Harems are exceptions now in modern Muslim societies plagued by economic problems. Polygamy is dying statistically,[27] but its assumptions are still at work even within monogamous households, as is illustrated by one of the interviews:

He keeps repeating that he will get a new wife. He threatens me every morning. I do not worry anymore. He is unable to support us. He cannot do anything anymore. How can he put up with one of those modern women? It would be a circus, but it hurts me when he says that, and I feel like hurting him back.

Maria M.

Muslim polygamy, thought of in general as a male privilege, does through a subtle institutional detail prevent the male from exercising his most intimate prerogative: the right to have intercourse with whichever wife he desires at a particular moment.

It is necessary for the polygamous husband to observe equality among his wives and not favor one at the expense of the others. If he leaves for a journey and he wants one of them to accompany him, he has to draw lots as the messenger used to do, and if he frustrates a wife from the night due to her, he should replace it by another night. This is a religious duty . . . The Prophet (upon him the *salut*) because of his noble sense of justice and his virile vigor used to have intercourse with all his other wives when he felt the desire to sleep with a woman who was not the one he was supposed to spend the night with according to the rotation system. That is how, according to Aicha [the youngest of the Prophet's wives and the one he loved the most], he performed such a task in one single night. According to Anas [*salut* upon him], the Prophet's *nine* wives received his conjugal visit in one single morning.[28]

The Prophet's sexual prowess was considered part of his outstanding personality. He was supposed to have the miraculous sexual vigor of forty men[29] but the ordinary believer is not expected to live up to the Prophet's example. Pragmatism is a Muslim quality and the strict application of the rotation system means, for the average man, who could not satisfy nine women in one morning, that he must refrain from giving in to sexual desire when it involves a woman not indicated by the rotation schedule. This insures scarcity in the midst of plenty. Not only does it oblige the male to scatter his emotional involvement, but it reinforces the rule of interchangeability. It obliges him to have intercourse with a woman he does not desire and forbids him from yielding to the attraction of another woman even though she is his own wife.

The underlying assumptions of polygamy are equally true for repudiation. Like polygamy, repudiation seems to be a male privilege allowing the man to change partners by the simple verbal pronunciation of the formula, ''I repudiate thee,'' but it is a boomerang. It works as much against the man as for him.

Letter 1

Fez, July 1971
Praise to God.
From Mr._____
To your highness the great religious scholar Mulay Mustapha Alaoui,
I am happy to come in front of your highness asking your advice concerning a catastrophe which has befallen me, a problem whose solution is beyond my capacity.
I pronounced the repudiation formula while I was boiling with anger. I pray your highness to tell me if there is anything I can do to have my wife back in spite of what has happened.
I must confess that I love my wife deeply and intensely.

Peace.

It is specified in the Moroccan code that a repudiation pronounced in anger or in drunkenness is not valid. Although this is quite well-known among average Moroccans, the husband seems to feel a need for reassurance in a society where words have such fatal importance. The husband's anxiety is echoed in the woman's fear of living in a state of illicitness with her own husband whenever he gives in to the temptation to use the repudiation formula.

Letter 2

Casablanca,
From Mrs._____
I had a quarrel with my husband and he repudiated me. Now I came back to him but he did not perform the legal formalities for our remarriage. Can I still stay with him or do I have to go to my parents' home? I have three children and he always keeps swearing, using the repudiation formula without ever performing the necessary acts to make our life lawful again. I have to add I married him very young. Do I have to put up with this situation or can I leave and go back to my parents?

Repudiation is not only a trap for the man and the woman, it morally binds all members of the family who feel uncomfortable when they have witnessed a verbal repudiation. If the man does not perform the legal remarriage, they feel that they are living with fornicators who engage in *zina*.

Letter 4

Province of Beni Mellal, 71-5-14
I am bringing to your attention this problem on behalf of Mr._____
A man said to his wife, "you are repudiated a triple repudiation" and he repeated it three times. It was a banal misunderstanding. He has children with his wife. She is still living with him in the house. He does not sleep with her or come near her or talk with her. But he still performs all his duties as a father: he gives her the money she needs for herself and for the children.
Now, given the fact that this man is an ignorant, that he does not have any knowledge about these religious matters, it is his father who is asking you about what

the religious laws say about this problem. Is there a way for this man to have his wife back or is not there any solution?

The striking thing about Moroccan divorce is that there is no check whatsoever on the desire of the husband to break the marital bond. The judge's role is limited to simply registering that desire — never contesting it.

The structural instability inherent in the Moslem family has been identified by psychiatrists[30] and pedagogues[31] as having disastrous effects on a child's development. This instability is likely to increase with the increasing pressures of modernization which create additional conflicts and tensions. A question like that of the woman's right to go outside of the home, which was unequivocally submitted to the husband's authorization in traditional households, is likely to become a source of confusion and conflict between husband and wife. Traditional patterns of heterosexual behavior, ideology, folk wisdom and law cannot be of any help to the male whose rights and privileges over his wife are challenged by modernization.

CHAPTER 7

The Mother-in-Law

In a traditional marriage, the mother-in-law is one of the strongest obstacles to conjugal intimacy. The close link between mother and son is probably the key factor in the dynamics of Muslim marriage. Sons, too involved with their mothers are particlarly anxious about their masculinity and wary of femininity.

Psychoanalytic theory has established the relationship with the mother as a determining factor in the individual's ability to handle a heterosexual relationship.[1] Cross-cultural studies like Phillip Slater's have shown that societies have used the effects of this relationship very efficiently. Phillip Slater divides societies according to the importance they place on the mother-son relationship:

> Societies vary between two poles, one of which accents the mother-child relationship, the other the marital bond. Each produces its own pattern of self-maintaining circularity . . .[2]

He establishes that in societies which institutionalize a weak marital bond, the mother-son relationship is accorded a particularly important place and vice-versa. In Muslim societies, not only is the marital bond actually weakened and love for the wife discouraged, but his mother is the only woman a man is allowed to love at all, and this love is encouraged to take the form of life-long gratitude.

> His mother beareth him with reluctance, and bringeth him forth with reluctance, and the bearing of him and the weaning of him is thirty months till, when he attaineth full strength and reacheth forty years, he saith, My Lord, arouse me that I may give thanks for the favor wherewith . . .[3]

The son's grateful love towards the mother is the object of many verses;[4] this one is symbolic in its conception of the relation as not being limited by time. It is not a process with a beginning, a middle and a ritualized end, indicating that now the adult male can engage in a new heterosexual relationship with his wife. On the contrary marriage, which in most societies is invested with a kind of initiation ritual function allowing the adult son to free himself from his mother, is in Moroccan Muslim society a ritual by which the mother's claim on the son is strengthened. Marriage institutionalizes the Oedipal split between love and sex in a man's life.[5] He is encouraged to love a woman he can't engage in sexual intercourse with, his mother. He is discouraged from lavishing his affection on the woman he does engage in sexual intercourse with, his wife.

THE MOTHER'S DECISIVE ROLE IN
THE CHOICE OF HER SON'S BRIDE

According to the interviews with traditional women, it is the mother, not the son, who initiates the marriage and carries out the decisions concerning the creation of her son's new family, although, officially, this is supposed to be the role of the father of the son.

> One day we were sitting in the courtyard as usual when somebody knocked at the door. An aunt of mine, the cousin of my father, who was to later become my *hma* ("mother-in-law") was at the door. She came straight from Tetuan. She was looking for a bride for her son . . . I was thirteen years old then. She saw me, talked with my father, asked him for my hand for her son and left. She came back two months later and my marriage contract was signed.
> (Did you know your husband?)
> No. I never talked to him.
>
> Fatiha F.

Appearances emphasize the role of the father-in-law who is responsible for the negotiations concerning the bride-price and the execution of financial decisions entailed by the marriage contract, but the mother's role is pivotal because she has access to information relevant to the marriage that only women have in a sexually segregated soceity. The mother is the one who can see the bride, engage in discussions with her and eventually acquire a very imtimate knowledge of her body. Only a woman in Moroccan society can see another woman nude and gather information concerning her health. This occurs in a *hammam* (a kind of turkish bath) which has manifold functions besides allowing a person to perform the purification rituals and bathe. The *hammam* is an intense communication center,[6] a powerful information agency, exposing the secrets of the families who frequent it.

The *guellassa* ("the cashier") and the *teyyaba* (the "girl friday" who assist the clientele with all sorts of things, giving massages, carrying water, suggesting herb recipes for uterine troubles) have a strategic position in the *hammam*. They have a more or less complete biographical account of the members of the families living around the *hammam*. The young girls are a particular target for gossip, and their behavior is a daily object of concern to the other women — those related to them and those who are not. A young girl's reputation has a direct impact on her family's honor and prestige. It is interesting to note that the women who are in charge of the making of the young girls' reputations, be they mother-in-laws, *guellassas, teyyabas,* or simply relatives of the son are all elderly women who no longer have sexual life, because they are widowed or divorced or simply abandoned by husbands involved with younger wives. The power of the elderly woman as both receiver and broadcaster of information concerning young women gives her tremendous power in deciding who is going to marry whom and reduces the man's decision-making role significantly. If the mother comes up with information about the bad breath of the future bride or a hidden physical deformity or a skin disease, she is likely to have a decisive influence on the matter. One such example was provided by Maria M., a fifty-five-year-old woman recalls that her marriage was postponed for seven years because the husband's mother told him that she suspected his future bride of having tuberculosis, given her extreme pallor and thin build. Because of the fathers of the bride and groom were close friends, such information could not break off the prospect of the marriage altogether, but it did have a mighty influence on the future bride's life:

> I was an old maid by everybody's standards when I got married. All my younger sisters were engaged and got married before me. My marriage became a kind of joke and I felt the object of divine curse. This is why I never open my mouth and say bad things when I am asked my opinion about a young girl. This happened years ago but I remember the humiliation vividly as if it happened yesterday. I still can not smile in the face of my husband's mother.
>
> Maria M.

The power of elderly women over the life course of young people is acknowledged by Moroccan folk wisdom which views the effects of age on men and women as having entirely opposite impacts:

> A man who reaches eighty becomes a saint;
> A woman who reaches sixty is on the threshold of hell.[7]

and again:

> What takes Satan a year to do
> Is done by the old hag within the hour.[8]

Advanced age for a woman is synonymous with the power to plot and intrigue:

> When the woman grows old
> She becomes obsessed with intrigues;
> Whatever she sees, she wants to get involved in,
> May God curse her, alive or dead.[9]

Before going any further, I should point out that even though the mother seems to be favored as a woman in Moroccan society, she does not escape the fate of being associated with the devil, the destructive force in the system. Elderly women, as is illustrated in the above proverbs, are viewed negatively, exactly like young women, by the society which endows them with a destructive potential. The only difference is that young women are destructive because they are sexually appealing, and old women are destructive because they can not claim sexual fulfillment anymore. Great pressures are put on the menopausal woman to regard herself as an asexual object and to renounce her sexuality as early as possible. Her husband is expected to turn his attention to younger women — so much so that a menopausal woman who tries to claim her sexual rights *vis-à-vis* her husband will be perceived as unrealistic and her complaints will be received with scepticism by both men and women. One of the current jokes which seems to have a lasting appeal for male Moroccan audiences is the following:

> Why doesn't the government create a kind of "used car dealership" for women where one can bring in the old wife, add some money and trade her in on a new one.

It is only by understanding the pressure on the aging woman to renounce her sexual self and her conjugal future, that one can understand the passion with which she gets involved in her son's life.

> In societies where sex antagonism is strong, the status of women low, and penis-envy therefore intense, the woman's emotional satisfactions will be sought primarily in the mother-son relationship; while in those societies in which these social characteristics are minimally present, the marital bond will be the principal avenue of need-gratification.[10]

In my data, all mother-in-laws were perceived as completely asexual. In a few cases where information about sleeping arrangements was available, the "old couple" although sharing the same room do not share the same bed.

THE MOTHER-IN-LAW AS FRIEND AND TEACHER

The mother-in-law and the wife should be considered competitors, but also as collaborators. The elderly woman has many things to offer the young, unexperienced bride, not only in matters concerning sex and pregnancy but also in other matters vital to a Moroccan woman's life such as physical beauty. The following quotation illustrates this aspect of the relationship between wife and mother-in-law:

> You see, with all that she did to me, with all her tyranny, I remember my mother-in-law with peace. I do not feel any resentment towards her. With time I came to see her in a more complex way. I realize now how complex a person she was . . . For example, she was very elegant, always dressed up and seated with a lot of poise and majesty, with her jewelry and her neat headgear. Clean and smart . . . She always

wanted us to be elegant, well-dressed, so that people would not say that she had sloppy brides . . . She was terribly refined.

Fatiha F.

And the secrets of refinement, elegance and adornment are valuable secrets in a society which emphasizes the importance of physical beauty and values the aristocratic *savior-vivre* of the urbanite. An important part of knowledge society bequeathes to the female child is the vast and diverse techniques and recipes for the use of plants, flowers, seeds, and minerals to make facials, shampoos, and cosmetics. Most Moroccan women still use these traditional beauty techniques in spite of the availability of cheap Western make-up. The mother-in-law's role as initiator in matters of *savoi-vivre* is as important as her role as instructress in matters of birth, sickness and death.

Moroccan marriage is virilocal. The child-wife leaves her family, either before or immediately after menarche, to live in her husband's household. She is often fearful of men — given her segregated upbringing — and thus more inclined to trust and to communicate with women. During her first conjugal years she is likely to have a deeper relationship with mother than with son:

I stayed with my husband until I had my first period.

(How long did you stay with your husband before you had your first period?)

I don't remember exactly — a year, maybe. I had no breasts, nothing. I was like a boy.

(Did he use to approach you?)

Never. He never approached me until after a whole year.

(And you were living with him and sharing the same room?)

I was living with my *hma* ("mother-in-law"); I used to cover myself every time I saw him.

(You were living with your *hma.*)

I was living with my *hma.* She used to treat me like a child of hers. She used to go to fetch young girls from the neighborhood to play with and talk with, so that I didn't feel bored.

Kenza

Moroccan parents are reluctant to give their daughters to husbands who live in different localities for fear of mistreatment. Usually, these fears are allayed if the mother of the groom decides to live with her son. To the bride's parents, distrustful of the husband, the presence of the mother-in-law seems to guarantee their daughter's fair treatment.

The following case of a husband-son from the province of Berkane provides an illustration — strange even by Moroccan standards — of the extent to which a mother may become involved in her daughter-in-law's business.

Province of Berkane, 20-V-71
To Moulay Mustapha Alaoui:
Dear Sir,

> I am the father of three children, all of whom were breast-fed *regularly* by my mother who lost her husband — i.e., my father — a long time ago. She did that because she had milk in her breast.
> What does religious law stipulate about this breast-feeding?

Not all mothers-in-law are gifted with the lacteous potential of the one above and the take-over of conjugal affairs need not be this extreme. It usually takes the form of the mother-in-law's assistance of the young bride during her first several pregnancies.

The interviews reveal that pregnancy is experienced as the submission of the woman's body to strange forces. One could almost speak of dissociative reflexes in women's perceptions of their swollen bodies:

> I became pregnant while still a child myself. I did not want people to see my belly. I wanted to hide it. I would sit so that people would not notice it. I spent whole days crying — just lying about and crying.[8]
>
> Kenza

> I did not know what was happening when the child started moving inside my belly. I would start screaming every time it happened. I had the impression that he was trying to come out of my skin. I felt very strange.
>
> Hayat H.

The perception of first pregnancies as pertaining to the realm of the bizarre is heightened by unpredictable miscarriages:

> I did not have my period during the first months that I was married. I was pregnant — a strange pregnancy. By the eighth month my belly was very swollen — a strange feeling, as if it were only fat . . . strange pregnancy. One day, I felt the labor, the pain. I had a hemorrhage that lasted for days. I told the people around me that I felt as though a frog was jumping in me, eating my heart. They answered, "It is nothing. You are just too young to know and be patient with pregnancy. What you feel is natural for women." I was not convinced. My husband took me to a doctor. She was a woman. She gave me shots right in by belly. After that I felt very odd and started shivering. Whatever was in my belly was dead. It started coming out. It was not a child. It was a strange accumulation of strange odd pieces.
>
> (Odd pieces?)
>
> Yes, pieces with strange shapes. It was not a child, but odd and different pieces. There were seven in all. One piece was like a fish, another like a grape, a white grape. Another was like an artichoke head; when you pushed on it a white head came out like an egg.
>
> Fatina F.

For the first years of marriage, the bride perceives her life as a succession of pregnancies and later recalls these years as being ones during which she was entirely devoted to her children and their problems: *"Kunt haida flwlad,"* is a sentence which comes often: "I was preoccupied with children." The mother-in-law emerges during these first years as a beneficent supervisor whose assistance allows the household to function efficiently. We will analyze the form of this assistance and its effect on the power structure of the domestic unit. We will focus our analysis on the case of Fatiha F., a forty-five year old wife and mother married to a *petit fonctionnaire*, whose job with the Ministry of Justice has required him to live in different parts of Morocco.

THE MOTHER-IN-LAW'S CONTROL OVER THE HOUSEHOLD:

The wife's submission to the mother-in-law is required by modern law which obliges her to "show deference towards the mother and father and close relatives of the husband."[11] Given the fact that a Moroccan household is often deserted by males, the only person the wife has to confront daily is the mother-in-law. This submission is usually expressed through two rituals: the hand-kissing ceremony and the duty of the wife to call her mother-in-law *Lalla* ("my mistress").

> . . . I did not tell the best of it all, the hand-kissing ceremony. We [the son's wives] had to kiss her hand twice a day, in the morning and after sunset. You kiss her hand on both sides of course. And we had to call her *Lalla*. When I sometimes forgot that hand, the world was turned upside down. She would engineer a whole show. She would not say anything to me directly to remind me of my duties. Oh no! That was too crude, not subtle enough for her. When my husband came home, she would attack him "Do you know something," she would say, "your wife is getting insolent. I have to put up with her insolence in silence because I love you and I don't want to create problems." "Mother," my husband would ask, "what did she do?" "Son, today she forgot to kiss my hand at sunset. She is taking more and more liberties with the rules."
>
> Fatiha F.

These deference ceremonies express the power allocation within the domestic unit. The symbol of that power is the key to the storage room where staples and food are kept. The person who has the key is the one who decides what and when to eat.

> My *hma* was in charge of everything. She had the power to decide what to eat, the quality and quantity, and she had the key. I could not use food except with her permission. We did the cooking of course. But once the food was ready we were not allowed to touch it. She would come into the kitchen and distribute it according to her own set of priorities. For example, on the eve of festivals we would spend nights making cookies. But we were not allowed to take any for our own use, not even for

our own children. Everything was stored by her. I could not even have a cup of tea if I felt like it aside from ritual meal times. I had to beg her for a piece of sugar and some twigs of mint [Moroccan tea is concocted of green tea, fresh mint and sugar.]

Fatiha F.

Goffman isolated a few variables in the power structure of total institutions. One of them is that the managers of the institutions make it impossible for the managed to obtain simple daily things such as cigarettes or a cup of tea or coffee, without submitting themselves to the humiliating process of soliciting permission.[12] In the Moroccan household, besides begging for food, the wife must ask for permission and money in order to go to the *hammam*. (The *hammam* is a semi-public institution whose normal price does not exceed twenty cents.) On such occasions, bickering and subtle blackmailing on the part of the mother-in-law might occur.

My *hma* was the treasurer, a very whimsical one too. Sometimes I would go to her and express my intention of visiting the *hammam*. However, before asking I would make sure that my husband had already given her the money for it. She would wait until I had prepared everything [it is a lengthy process involving the preparation of facials and home made shampoos, etc.] I would put on my *djellaba*, veil my face and go to her. She would then change her mind and say, "Do you really have to go? Can't you heat water and bathe here?" I would take off my *djellaba*, take off my veil and sit down without uttering a word, no protest. I could not protest. To protest, you have to have somebody's support; you have to have your parents' support. I did not have that. So I thanked God for the fate he chose for me and shut my mouth.

Fatiha F.

The competition between mother and wife towards the son's favors is clearly institutionalized by the son's duty to give to his mother whatever he gets for his wife.

My husband could not give me a gift. Suppose he wanted to give me a scarf. He would say, "F_____, I would like to see you in a red scarf, it will match your complexion." I would answer that I would be very happy to have one. He would go to the store, but he would have to buy four scarves — one for his mother, two for his divorced sisters and, finally, one for me. He couldn't give me the red scarf directly, he had to give them to his mother. She then chose what she wanted for herself and her daughters and gave me the last one. It could be green or black.

Fatiha F.

My husband could not come near me before going to salute his mother. Once he wanted to surprise me. He bought me a bra and hid it in his pocket before going to greet his mother. She noticed that he had something in his pocket and she laughingly took the bra out of his pocket and ridiculed him: "I did not know that you started using a bra, like a woman. She [the wife] has eaten your brain. You act like a crazy man now [to get things for the wife only]. Where did you drink it? [The reference is to witchcraft done by the wife to make her husband love her.] Did you drink it in the soup? Or was it discreetly mixed in your cookies?

This sort of incident is a favorite subject for playwrights in Morocco. One of the most despised personages in the popular theater is the mother-in-law.

The mother's involvement with her son, in a traditional setting, is not limited to material things. It goes so far as to prevent his being alone with his wife. There is no way for husband and wife to be together during the day without being conspicuously anti-social.

The social space in a family dwelling is centered on one focal room, *al-bit al-kbir* ("the big room"). Here everything happens and it is here that everyone is encouraged to spend most of their time. Individual privacy is vehemently discouraged. One of the accepted gestures for showing dissent within the family is to refuse to come to this communal room, to shut oneself off in another room. Leaving the communal room right after dinner is considered especially rude in traditional households. It is therefore "natural" for the mother-in-law to use this custom to keep her son with her for as long as possible.

Often late in the evening, I felt very sleepy, but I could not leave the communal room to go to sleep in mine. Neither could my husband, even if both of us were literally dying of fatigue. We still had to sit there with her and wait until she decided to go to bed. Then we would run to ours. I could not retire to my room before her. We could not close our door in her face.

(And what if it is your husband who takes the initiative to go to bed?)

Impossible. He can't. You want her to explode? When he used to come very early to the house after work, she would turn to him and say, "Why did you come home so early? Isn't there any fun in the streets? Aren't there women in the streets? Aren't there amusements? Cinemas? Why do you have to come home so early? Men should not be always near their wives. It is a very ugly habit." Often we go to sleep and I can hear her roaming around the windows, trying to listen to our noises, in case I was trying to tell him what happened during the day. I was not crazy enough to tell him secrets, knowing that she was spying on us. One day I forgot to shut the window properly. So when she leaned on it, the door went ajar under her weight.

(Did she ever try to join you in bed?)

Not in our own house, but when we were invited to go somewhere, we spent the night together in the same room.

Fatiha F.

When the couple decides to leave the extended family, they often seek "a government decision to transfer as an escape if the man is a civil servant, thus hiding their desire for privacy under a legitimate cloak. The wife perceives the government's decision to transfer the husband to another locality as an opportunity to recover some power over her life and her husband, and the mother-in-law perceives such a decision as a plot against her.

My husband was busy trying to get us out of there [the extended family, which included the father, the father's brother's family, and two of his sons' families]. He was lobbying to have himself transferred to another part of the country by government decision. It was the only solution compatible with his obedience and respect for his mother.

He lobbied so well that the got his transfer. He was ordered to go to Fedala. But he had to disclose the news to his mother. One day he decided to talk to her. He told her that he was forced by the government to go to Fedala [forty miles away] and that he had no choice but to follow the government decision if he was to keep his job. "Are you joking?" she said, "You don't have to leave us. You can commute. Many people commute. It does not seem to kill them. Don't mention leaving. That is out of the question." He then came to me and said, "Fatiha, look. Do you want to leave this house at any cost?" "Yes," I said. "Listen," he said. "This is our only chance to escape. I am not going to wait any longer. I am going to speed up the transfer decision. I am going to rent a room, any room. I do not want to hear you complain about how ugly that room might be, or how rough life is going to be for us. And it is going to be financially tough for a long period. Are you ready to put up with that without complaining?" "Any slum," I whispered, "will be a castle for us alone."

He came one day very late and managed to isolate himself with me and whispered, "Start packing. We are going to leave very soon. I will announce it at the last moment, so as to take her by surprise. Start packing very discreetly."

I can't tell you what I felt then. I lost my appetite. I lost my tongue. It was both joy and fear. Have you ever experienced joy and fear together? I fasted two days. I could not eat with that secret within me. I did not know anymore how to behave, how to walk, what to say. He left the house and left me alone. I lost the sense of conventions. He was counting on me to pack. I did just the opposite. Instead of packing, I went and opened the carpet which was rolled in a corner. I took my precious drapes [used only during festival days] and hung them on the door. When he came that night he looked puzzled. He came to me and whispered, looking at the drapes and the carpet, "Fatiha, are you crazy? What does this mean. I told you to pack."

"It means," I answered, "that I don't know anything about your decision, that I am out of it." I was scared his mother would discover that we were plotting. I did not let him down really. But it was the only possible and sensible thing to do, although it seemed then as if I was letting him down. "I don't know anything," I kept repeating to him. Poor thing, he was left alone to face his mother.

The following day he came in shouting at me, screaming with a very loud voice you could hear from the mosque, "Fatiha, you have to pack immediately. These dogs of the government have given me the order to spend the night at Fedala. I do not have the right to refuse anymore. Immediately! Do you hear, Fatiha?"

"But," shouted his mother from her room, "Where will you spend the night. You have a family. They can't treat you that way. You can't stay in the street."

"Mother," he said. "They have foreseen everything. They made it impossible for me to defer any longer the transfer decision. They provided me with a house and a truck to transport the luggage. The truck is coming within the hour."

The anti-privacy structure of Moroccan society facilitates — indeed, almost requires — the mother-in-law's intervention in her son's physical intimacy with his wife. Recognizing this, we can avoid falling into the Moroccan prejudice against old women, cursed as "intrigue masters." It is the structure which sets up the roles for everyone and leaves specific outlets for the human individual's cravings and wishes. It is the structure which is vicious, not the mother-in-law.

The triangle of mother son and wife is the trump card in the Muslim pack of legal, ideological and physical barriers which subordinate the wife to the husband and condemn the heterosexual relation to mistrust, violence and deceit. Young people demanding love-marriages not only create tremendous conflicts with their parents, they also almost guarantee conflict in their own marriages. Given the way they have been brought up, the traditional patterns of sexual relatedness in their society, and the government's lack of support, they are almost sure to fail in their effort to create a fulfilling heterosexual relationship based on love rather than conflict.

The traditional pattern for heterosexual relations is being destroyed before meaningful alternative patterns of relatedness can develop. Traditionally sexuality was controlled by separating the sexes spatially, but modern sexual desegregation is swiftly eroding those spatial boundaries.

CHAPTER 8

The Meaning of Spatial Boundaries

Muslim sexuality is a territorial one, i.e., a sexuality whose regulatory mechanisms consist primarily of a strict allocation of space to each sex and an elaborate ritual for resolving the contradictions arising from the inevitable interferences between spaces.[1] Apart from the ritualized trespasses of women into public spaces which are, by definition, male spaces, there are no accepted patterns for interactions between unrelated men and women. Such interactions violate the space rules which are the pillars of the Muslim sexual order.

Institutionalized boundaries dividing parts of the society express the recognition of power in one part at the expense of the other.[2] Any transgression of the boundaries is a danger to the social order because it is an attack on the acknowledged allocation of power. The link between boundaries and power is particularly salient in a society's sexual patterns.

> Patterns of sexual dangers can be seen to express symmetry or hierarchy. It is impossible to interpret them as expressing something about the actual relation of the sexes. I suggest that many ideas about sexual dangers are better interpreted as symbols of the relation between parts of society, as mirroring designs of hierarchy or symmetry which apply in the larger social system.[3]

The symbolism of sexual patterns certainly seems to reflect the society's hierarchy and power allocation in the Muslim order. Strict space boundaries divide Moroccan society into two sub-universes: the universe of men, the *Umma* universe of religion and power and the universe of women, the domestic universe of sexuality and the family. The spatial division according to sex reflects the division between those who hold authority and those who do not, those who hold spiritual powers and those who do not.[4] The division is based on the physical separation of the *Umma* and the domestic universe. These two universes[5] of social interaction are regulated according to antithetical concepts of human relations, one based on community, the other on conflict:

Membership

The Public Universe of the UMMA
Members: the believers. Women's position in the *Umma* universe is ambiguous; Allah does not talk to them. We can therefore assume that the *Umma* is primarily male believers.

The Domestic Universe of Sexuality
Members: Individuals of both sexes as primarily sexual beings. But because men are not supposed to spend their time in the domestic unit, we could assume that the members are, in fact, women only.

Principles Regulating Relations Between Members

Umma	The Family
Equality	Inequality
Reciprocity	Lack of Reciprocity
Aggregation	Segregation
Unity, Communion	Separation, Division
Brotherhood, Love	Subordination, Authority
Trust	Mistrust

COMMUNAL RELATIONSHIP

A social relationship will be so-called 'communal' if and so far as the orientation of social action is based on subjective feeling of the parties, whether affectual or traditional, that they belong together.[6]

The universe of the *Umma* is communal ; its citizens are persons who unite in a democratic collectivity based on a sophisticated concept of belief in a set of ideas, which is geared to produce integration and cohesion of all members who are participating in the unifying task.

CONFLICT RELATIONSHIP

A social relationship will be referred to as a 'conflict' in so far as action within it is oriented intentionally to carrying out the actor's own will against the resistance of the other party or parties.[7]

The citizens of the sexuality universe are primarily sexual beings, they are not united but rather are divided into two categories of individuals, strictly defined according to sex, which division justifies the granting of denial of priveleges. This universe is based on sexual segregation and the subordination of one sex to the other. Women, members of the domestic universe, are subject to the authority of men, members of the *Umma* universe. Separation and subordination are embodied in instituions which enforce non-communication and non-interaction between the members of each universe. Members do not partake in any unifying task together (except procreation). In fact whenever the interaction of men and women is inevitable, as for procreation, the universe of sexuality has a host of mechanisms to limit that interaction and to prevent the growth of intimacy. Sexual segregation pervades all aspects of life.

THE SECLUSION OF WOMEN

In order to prevent sexual interaction between members of the Umma and members of the domestic universe, seclusion and veiling (a symbolic form of seclusion) were implemented. But, paradoxically, sexual segregation heightens the sexual dimension of any heterosexual interaction.

In a country like Morocco, heterosexual encounter is the focus of so much restriction, and consequently attention, that seduction becomes a structural component of the culture. Seduction is a conflict strategy, a way of winning without giving of yourself. Seduction games are the only way to relate in a culture where other heterosexual interaction is prevented.

The hedonistic enhancement of the beauty of the human body seems to have been a strong Mediterranean characteristic of Morocco which Islam failed to curb. Body adornment with both jewelry and cosmetics is an integral part of socialization. Even men, at least the generation now in their sixties, used to wear cosmetics to darken their eyelids (*khol*) and lips (*swak*) for religious rituals and festivals. Islam took an unequivocally negative attitude towards body ornamentation, especially for women.[8] It required pious women to be modest in their appearance and hide all ornamentation and eye-catching beauty behind veils.

> And tell the believing women to lower their gaze and be modest, and to display of their adornment only that which is apparent and to draw their veils over their bosoms, and not to reveal their adornment save to their own husbands or fathers or husband's fathers, or their sons or their husband's sons, or their women, or their slaves, or male attendants who lack vigor or children who know naught of women's nakedness. And let them not stamp their feet so as to reveal what they hide of their adornment. And turn unto Allah together, O believers, in order that ye may succeed.[9]

According to Ghazali, the eye is undoubtedly an erogenous zone in the Muslim structure of reality, as able to give pleasure as the penis. A man can do as much damage to a woman's honor with his eyes as if he were to seize hold of her with his hands.

> To look at somebody else's wife is a sinful act . . . The look is fornication of the eye, but if the sexual apparatus is not set in motion by it [i.e., if the man does not attempt to have sexual intercourse], it is a much more easily pardoned act . . .[10]

When the Prophet was asking God to protect him from the most virulent social dangers, he asked Allah to help him control his penis and his eye from the dangers of fornication.[11]

The theory that seclusion in Islam is a device to protect the passive male who cannot control himself sexually in the presence of lust-inducing female is further substantiated by verse 60 of Surah 24 which explains that elderly women (supposed to be unattractive) can go unveiled. The Belghiti survey of rural women, among whom seclusion is the prevailing mode, reveals that the restrictions on women's movements do not apply to elderly women, who consequently have a greater freedom.[13]

The seclusion of women, which to Western eyes is a source of oppression, is seen by many Muslim women as a source of pride.[14] The traditional women interviewed all perceived seclusion as prestigious. In rural Morocco seclusion is considered the privilege of women married to rich men.[15]

Harems, the ultimate form of seclusion, were considered even more prestigious since they require huge economic assets. One of the women I interviewed, Salama, lived most of her life as a concubine in a harem. This is unusual even by Moroccan standards, and her experience contrasts sharply with that of most women. Because women are not allowed to leave a harem, sexual segregation is more successfully realized there than in the average, monogamous family. Successful seclusion of human beings requires considerable economic investment because services must be provided at home for the secluded. Other women, who must go out to shop or go to the baths, are under many restrictions outside the home.

THE DESECLUSION OF WOMEN: ON THE STREET

Traditionally, women using public spaces, trespassing on the Umma universe, are restricted to few occasions and bound by specific rituals,[16] such as the wearing of the veil. The veil is worn by Moroccan women only when they leave the house and walk through the street, which is a male space. The veil means that the woman is present in the men's world, but invisible; she has no right to be in the street.

If chaperoned, women are allowed to trespass into the men's universe on the traditional visits to the *Hammam*, "the public bath," and to the tomb of the local saint. According to my data, the visit to the *Hammam* used to be bi-monthly and that to the saint's tomb not more than once or twice a year (usually the 27th day of Ramadan) and both required the husband's permission. The chaperoning was entrusted to an elderly asexual woman, usually the mother-in-law.

Traditionally, only necessity could justify the woman's presence outside the home, and there was never any respect attached to poverty and necessity. Respectable women were not seen on the street. In class-conscious Morocco the maid, who has to go wherever she can find a job, occupies the lowest end of the social scale, and to be called a maid is one of the commonest insults. Only whores or insane women wandered freely in the streets. One expression for a whore is *Rajlha Zahqa,* "a woman whose foot is slipping." The Pascon-Bentahar survey revealed that when a rural youth visits a town he assumes that any woman walking down the street is sexually available.[17]

Women in male spaces are considered both provocative and offensive. Since schooling and jobs both require women to be able to move freely through the streets, modernization necessarily exposes many women to public harassment.

In *The Hidden Dimension,* Edward Hall made two perceptive remarks about space use in Middle-Eastern, Arabo-Muslim, societies. First, "there is no such thing as an intrusion in public. Public means public." [18] It is not possible for an individual to claim a private zone in a public space. This seems quite true for Morocco and has a particular bearing on woman's presence in the street, as one might guess.

The second remark is that space has a primarily social rather than physical quality. The notion of trespassing is not so much related to physical boundaries as it is to the identity of the person performing the act.[19] A friend for example never trespasses, while a foe always does.

A woman is always trespassing in a male space because she is, by definition, a foe. A woman has no right to use male spaces. If she enters them, she is upsetting the male's order and his peace of mind. She is actually committing an act of aggression against him merely by being present where she should not be. A woman in a traditionally male space upsets Allah's order by inciting men to commit *zina.* The man has everything to lose in this encounter: peace of mind, self-determination, allegiance to Allah and social prestige.

If the woman is unveiled the situation is aggravated. The Moroccan term for a woman who is not veiled is *aryana* ("nude"), and most women who frequent schools or hold jobs outside the home are unveiled today. Both elements together — trespassing and trespassing in the "nude" — constitute an open act of exhibitionism.

> Whether the indictable act consists of words spoken, gestures covered, or act performed, the communication structure of the event often consists of an individual initiating an engagement with a stranger of the opposite sex by means of the kind of message that would be proper only if they were on close and intimate terms. Apart from psychodynamic issues, exhibitionists often spectacularly subvert social control that keeps individuals interpersonally distant even though they are physically close to each other. The assault here is not so much directly on an individual as on the system of rights and symbols the individual employs in expressing relatedness and unrelatedness to those about him. [20]

The male's response to the woman's presence is, according to the prevailing ideology, a logical response to an exhibitionist assault. It consists in pursuing the woman for hours, pinching her if the occasion is propitious, eventually assaulting her verbally, all in the hope of convincing her to carry out her exhibitionist propositioning to its implied end.

During the Algerian revolution, the Nationalist movement used women to carry arms and messages. One of the problems the revolutionary movement was faced with was the harrassment of these women by Algerian "brothers" who mistook them for prostitutes and interfered with the performance of their nationalist task.[21] A similar incident was reported to have taken place near a refugee camp in Lebanon.

A female Palestinian militant was performing her task as a sentinel. She was posted in a deserted spot a few yards away from the camp, her machine-gun on her shoulder, when a Lebanese civilian who noticed her came by to make a proposition. When the woman rejected his advances with indignant words and gestures, the man got angry and said, "How do you want me to believe that a woman standing alone in the street the whole night has any honor?" The woman is said to have turned her gun towards her suitor and told him, "I am here in the street soiling my honor to defend yours because you are unable to do it yourself."[22] In spite of its revolutionary setting, the anecdote reveals that the female militant shares with the male civilian the belief that her being alone in the street was dishonorable. Her reflex was to justify her presence in the male space, not to claim her right to be there.

THE DESECLUSION OF WOMEN: IN THE OFFICE

The absence of modes of relatedness other than genital encounter helps to explain the form of heterosexual encounters in offices as well as on the street.

The office is a recent development in Moroccan history, a legacy of the centralized bureaucracy set up by the French after 1912. After independence, the public administration expanded both in terms of offices and posts and in terms of the portion of the public resources it swallows. Presently the state is by far the most important employer in the country. A substantial number of the literate working women are in government offices. These women, who often have not finished high school, are typists and secretaries and usually occupy subordinate positions *vis-à-vis* males.

The situation of the working woman in the office is reminiscent of her position in a traditional household and on the street. These conflicting images are likely to stimulate conflicting patterns of behavior in the man. The boss's typist, like his wife and sister, is in a subordinate position, and he has the right to command her. Like them, she is dependent on him (more or less directly) for economic survival. He administers her salary, which is given to her because she provides specific services to him. The confusion between the individual and his role in the office is one of the serious problems of modern management, but confusion about changing roles for men and women is evident in all areas of public life.

Women's increasing use of traditionally male spaces greatly intensifies the sexual aspect of any encounter between men and women, especially in urban centers. Modernization demands the breakdown of the traditional sexual segregation in order to use women in the production process. Women must have the right to walk throught the streets in order to get to their work. And more and more women are going to work.

Not only are women trespassing on the universe of the *Umma* when they go to work, but they are also competing with men for the few available jobs. The anxiety created by women working, taking on a traditionally male role, is intensified by the scarcity of jobs and the high unemployment rate.

CHAPTER 9

The Economic Basis of Sexual Anomie
in Modern Morocco

One can easily imagine the problems likely to result from the gradual integration of women into the labor force in a country, like Morocco, suffering from acute unemployment.[1] A society which has difficulty providing enough jobs for its men will tend to define women as having no economic function outside the family. This is precisely the case with the Moroccan *Code* which reflects Islam's traditional status of women in order to deny women's claim on, and access to, the labor market. On the other hand, within the family, the same economic necessities often make it imperative for the woman to find a job in order to supplement her husband's income. This conflict is a major cause of the anomie pervading male-female relationships in economically depressed Morocco.

Anomie, according to Durkheim, is more a confusion of norms than the absence of norms. Anomie occurs at times when:

> The moral system which has prevailed for centuries is shaken, and fails to respond to new conditions of human life, without any new system having yet been formed to replace that which has disappeared.[2]

In the case of Moroccan male-female dynamics, sexual desegregation, through schooling and employment of women in non-domestic jobs, is a direct attack on the spatial barrier Islam erected between males and females. But Islam's division of space between the sexes is not an isolated phenomenon, it is the reflection of a specific distribution of power and authority and of a specific division of labor which together form a coherent social order. Moroccan society has not pushed its social reform in matters of male-female relations as far as the changes in the traditional distribution of power and authority might have warranted; whence the anomic aspect of that relation.

The role of the Moroccan government appears more clearly if we contrast it to another traditional society, China, which underwent an entirely different process of change affecting both reality and ideology. During the phase of nationalist struggle (i.e., struggle against external hegemony), Mao Tse Tung analyzed the Chinese situation thus:

89

> A man in China is usually subjected to the dominations of three systems of authority: 1) the State system (political authority); 2) the clan system (clan authority); and 3) the supernatural system (religious authority) . . . As for women, in addition to being dominated by these three systems of authority, they are also dominated by the men (the authority of the husband). These four authorities . . . are the four thick ropes binding the Chinese people . . .[3]

One of the first acts of independent China was the promulgation, on May 1, 1950, of the Marriage Law of the People's Republic of China whose first article states:

> The arbitrary and compulsory feudal marriage system which is based on the superiority of men over women and which ignores the children's interests is abolished.

The Chinese man is not burdened by the duty to support his wife as well as himself. The Chinese woman is not limited to biological reproduction and sexual services. She is urged to earn her own living as a productive economic agent. Consequently, the Chinese male is encouraged not to think of himself only as a sexual being, but primarily as an economic agent and as a person with multiple potentials and capacities.

Change is a painful process, but it becomes bearable to the individual if the degree of ambiguity and contradiction is lessened by the availability of coherent new models for behavior.[4] The Chinese husband suffers less than the Moroccan husband because the former at least knows exactly what new attitude he is expected to have towards his wife's work:

> Both husband and wife shall have the right to free choice of occupation and free participation in work or in social activities.[5]

The Moroccan husband on the other hand is faced with anxiety-provoking ambiguities. This is epitomized in the Moroccan *Code's* decision concerning the man's right to control his wife's access to the outside world. It is a masterpiece of ambiguities and a potential goldmine of congugal discord. In traditional Morocco, the man's prestige is embodied in the seclusion of his female relatives. A man whose wife wanders around in the streets free, is a man whose masculinity is in jeopardy. Article 35 of the Modern *Code* states that among the woman's rights *vis-à-vis* her husband is the right to visit her parents, implying that she has no other right to leave the house without her husband's permission. Although sexual equality was proclaimed in the Moroccan constitution in the name of equality between all citizens, the right to leave the house and thus by implication the right to work outside the home, (which assumes a particular importance in a traditionally segregated setting), were not granted by Moroccan legislators to the female citizen. On the contrary, the need for the woman to negotiate such rights with her husband is emphasized.

Since the system holds as a law that the woman's place is in the home and that her access to offices and factories is subordinated to her husband's authorization, the woman is reminded whenever she gets a job that it is a privilege and not a right. Moreover the husband is encouraged to perceive his wife and her salary as belonging to him since she requires his permission in order to earn her salary. (In fact, in spite of the 1957 *Code's* uncompromising stand on the separation of properties and on the woman's uncontested right to manage her own property, the husband's claim to his wife's salary is a recurrent subject of dispute in Moroccan courts.[7])

One can imagine the frustration and resentment the Moroccan male is likely to experience, cornered between a law which gives him the right to control his wife's moves and the economic necessity which forces her to take a job. The gap between the sexual ideology reflected by the laws and that apparent in most people's lives is the sign of the absence of a genuine modern Moroccan moral system.

The nationallist movement which initiated and supported changes in the woman's position in society has failed to carry out its post-independence task of socio-economic regeneration. Whatever the reasons, the unfortunate destiny of the Nationalist movement had disastrous implications for both sexual desegregation and the prospects of an integrated women's liberation, where ideology and reality reflect each other in a coherent structure. The present situation is characterized by a flagrant discrepancy between women's newly acquired rights to use traditionally male spaces such as streets, offices, and classrooms, and the traditional ideology according to which such rights are clear cases of trespass.

EDUCATION FOR WOMEN

Education for women has been a major factor in sexual desegregation. It is associated with Westernization, but it would be a mistake to attribute it just to French influence.[8] The French policy, inspired by General Lyautey, who liked to think of himself as a great humanist and philosopher, was respect for Moroccan traditions whenever they were not in open contradiction to the French interests. For example, the traditional land-owning system conflicted with French interests and was entirely dismantled while the Moroccan family structure, which did not conflict, became the object of an exotic respect.

The introduction of schooling for girls cannot be explained without taking into account the renaissance-like nationalist movement which swept Morocco's urban centers in the 1930's and 1940's. Nationalists held a particularly optimistic belief in Morocco's ability to rejuvenate its structures, re-vitalize itself, shake off useless anachronisms and bridge the centuries which separated it from the industrial world. Schooling for women, unthinkable a few decades before, was advocated by the nationalists as a necessity by 1942. They wanted to defeat the French at any cost, even if it meant interfering in the family's structure.

Under these circumstances Moroccan girls were pushed into classrooms, entrusted to the hands of male teachers and allowed to walk through the streets four times a day. All of these events were indeed unusual, but everything was unusual in Morocco in 1942.

> Finally, on the second of the month of Moharram in the year 1362 [that is November 1942 of the Christian calendar] a Moroccan delegation was received by His Majesty and was given a most warm welcome. He himself saw no problem in allowing men to teach Arabic to Muslim girls. Some days later there was a gathering of young people from Fez, Rabat, and Sale at the Palace where His Majesty was presiding at the Council of Ministers. These young people were admitted to participate in the discussions of the issue at hand. The meeting lasted two hours and the following decisions were made: age for entering school [for girls] 7 years of age; for leaving school 13 years. For the program of primary education for girls, teachers of Arabic were chosen and designated directly by His Majesty.[9]

The "young people" who went to see the King about the matter of girls' education were nationalist militants, and "His Majesty" was Mohammad V, who puzzled the whole country in 1943 when he presented his daughter, Princess Aicha, unveiled in front of the nation. The liberation of women was considered by the Nationalists as an absolutely necessary step in the strategy to beat the French Christians.

The Nationalist leader, Allal al-Fasi, did not forget women when he was participating in the drafting of an "Arab Charter" during the same period:

> The state must provide gratuitously a basic minimum in the following spheres:
> a—maternity, motherhood, child care . . .
> The state must ensure to individuals the following rights in the field of production:
> c—. . . enabling women to perform their duties in society.[10]

The number of girls in primary schools rose from 15,080 in 1947,[11] to 186,330 in 1957, and to 423,005 in 1971.[12] The movement for women's education apparently snowballed, because, starting in 1945, girls did not stop going to school at the age thirteen as had been decided by the Nationalists; they had gained access to secondary schools. Seven percent of Moroccan girls between ages 14 and 19 are in secondary establishments now; the percentage of boys is 14 percent.[13] According to government figures, 92,006 girls were enrolled in secondary schools in 1971, and a token number of girls made it to the universities.[14]

Although the percentage of females in school is ridiculously low according to Western standards, it would be a mistake to dismiss it as insignificant. Since sexual segregation is primarily a symbolic spatial confinement of women, just a few women strolling along the streets in an unhurried fashion can upset the society's psychic equilibrium.

JOBS FOR WOMEN

The most important factor in desegregation is probably the number of working women, which exceeds two million according to a non-official commentary on the 1971 census.[16] Working women account for 25% of the female population, and 37% of the working class.[17]

I have recourse to a non-official document, because even according to the authors of the official data the female labor foce in Morocco is underestimated.[18] It would probably be more revealing to study the way the 1971 census dealt with women than to study the figures themselves, but I will content myself here with a brief review of the statistical data.

According to the official census, while the employment rate for men is rather stagnant, the women's rate has shown a tremendous increase. In the period between 1960 and 1971, this rate has increased 75%. In urban areas, where women's labor is more easily assessed, the number of working women has doubled.

> The women, encouraged on the one hand by socio-economic changes which are taking place, and on the other hand by a rising level of education, is becoming a serious competitor to men in the labor market. Out of every 100 active individuals, 30 are young women.[19]

The most striking characteristic of Moroccan female labor is its youth; 44% of the working women are less than twenty-five, and 15% are less than fifteen years old. The corresponding figures for men are 29% for those less than twenty-five, and 6% for those less than fifteen.

In the services sector there are predominantly two kinds of working women, the civil servant and the maid. There are 27,700 women working mainly for the Moroccan government, 15,200 of whom hold teaching jobs. The integration of women into prestigious activities such as teaching, health and finance, gains in saliency precisely because the bulk of working women are illiterate or semi-literate.

Lack of education forces most women into subordinate positions, under men's supervision, hardly different from their traditional situations. Maids for example occupy such a traditional subordinate position. They are remarkable not only for their numbers (100,200), but also for their age distribution — over half of the maids in Morocco are under twenty-five years old and 29% are less than fifteen. One of the ominous gifts of modernization, child labor, is due to many factors, but mainly to the disintegration of the traditional rural social structure coupled with the rapid increase in population.

Apart from civil servants and maids, women's participation in the economy is concentrated in four kinds of economic activities: agriculture, cattle-raising, the textile and ready-made clothes industries.

But given that the official documents define "economically active" so that it includes both people holding jobs and those looking for jobs, a thorough picture of the female labor situation can not be drawn without looking at female unemployment (see page 109). The number of people employed according to the official data has not risen since 1960, but the structure of unemployment by sex has registered a spectacular change. While the number of unemployed males remained unchanged, the number of women seeking jobs has multiplied by ten within eleven years. While female unemployment did not account for 2% of the total unemployment figure in 1960, it reached 21% in 1971. The absence of an institutionalized right to work predisposes women to fall prey to unemployment much more easily than their male colleagues.

The 1971 census defines women working within the household as inactive. 2,800,000 Moroccan housewives are considered to contribute nothing to society. And, as the census-takers admit, "in rural areas women's participation in economic activity is confused with housework, and a certain reticence on the part of the husband to declare his wife active was noticed."[20] In 1960 the number of women whose labor was under reported was estimated to be 1,200,000. A more accurate census would have inflated the number of unemployed people tremendously by adding the "under-estimated" female farm-workers.

The traditional definition of feminity would however have reassured us that the number of unemployed women was not as significant as that of men, since after all a woman's place is in the home. Because the woman's right to work is ambiguous, the state is only responsible to provide enough jobs for the men. Providing enough jobs for women becomes not an obligation but an act of benevolent generosity. Keeping women in the home under the control of men, satisfies both psychological and economic needs in a depressed economy.

THE FUNCTIONS OF SEXUAL REPRESSION IN A DEPRESSED ECONOMY

Less visible but probably more pernicious than the economic aspect is the psychological function of female oppression as an outlet for male frustration and aggression. Wilhelm Reich has drawn attention to the functions of the patriarchal family in economically depressed societies. He emphasizes that "economic freedom goes hand in hand with the dissolution of old institutions," particularly those "governing sexual policies,"[21] and that sexually frustrated males are less likely to rebel against economic exploitation:

> The suppression of one's primitive material needs compasses a different result than the suppression of one's sexual needs. The former incites to rebellion, whereas the latter — inasmuch as it causes sexual needs to be repressed — withdraws them from consciousness and anchors itself as a moral defense, prevents rebellion against both forms of suppression. Indeed the inhibition of rebellion itself is unconscious. In the consciousness of the average non-political man there is not even a trace of it.[22]

A sexually repressed male is preoccupied with symbols such as "purity" and "honor" because his experience of genital sexuality is "dirty" by his society's standards and, consequently, by his own standards. For example, the rural Moroccan youth whose sexual desires are savagely thwarted from their female goals so that he has to choose between sodomy, homosexuality, and masturbation, all equally condemned, is likely to be particularly sensitive to the ideas of honor and purity:

> The man who attains genital satisfaction is honorable, responsible, brave, and controlled without making much of a fuss about it. These attitudes are an organic part of his personality. The man whose genitals are weakened, whose sexual structure is full of contradictions, must continually remind himself to control his sexuality, to preserve his sexual dignity, to be brave in the face of temptations, etc. . . .[23]

Honor and purity, two particularly sensitive emotional concepts in Muslim North African society, link the man's prestige in an almost fatal way to the sexual behavior of the women under his charge, be they his wives, sisters, or unmarried female relatives.[24] A man who has a wife or sister working in an office or going to school is a man who runs a very serious chance of seeing "his honor soiled." He must face the real possibility of witnessing his prestige fall into pieces when one of his women is noticed "driving around with the boy next door" after school or office hours. To have men's honor embodied in women's sexual behavior was a much safer system when women's space was strictly confined to the courtyard and ritual visits to the *hammam* ("Turkish bath") or the local saint's tomb. It is no wonder that the women who have such tremendous power to maintain or destroy a man's position in society are going to be the focus of his frustrations and aggression.

Male frustration is likely to be aggravated by the differences in the ways men and women are socialized to handle sexual drives. Men are encouraged to expect full satisfaction of their sexual desires, and to perceive their masculine identity as closely linked to that satisfaction. Women are early taught to curb their sexual drives. Little girls are told in detail about the vagina and the uterus, and about the penis's "destructive" effects on these two parts of women's bodies. The *hammam*, where children bathe together with adults, is a normal place for questions and answers about human anatomy. A brother's circumcision at the age of five is also an occasion for little girls to ask questions. Moreover, grown-ups frequently do not wait until the child asks questions. They volunteer the information upon which the honor and prestige of the group depend.

The male child is introduced differently to sex. His penis, *htewta* ("little penis"), is the object of a real cult on the part of the women rearing him. Little sisters, aunts, maids, mothers, often attract the little boy's attention to his *htewta* and try to teach him to pronounce the word, which is quite a task given the gutteral initial letter "h." One of the common games played by adult females with a male child is to make him realize the connection between *sidi* ("master") and the *htewta*. *"Hada sidhum"* ("This is their master"), say the women, pointing to the child's penis. They try to make him repeat the sentence while pointing to his own penis. The kissing of the child's penis is a normal gesture of a female relative who has not seen him since his birth. *"Tbarkallah Al Ar-Rajal"* ("God protect the man"), she may whisper. In short, the child's phallic pride is enhanced systematically, beginning in the first years of life. And as the boy matures, the fact that men have privileges such as polygamy and repudiation which allow them not only to have multiple sexual partners but also to change partners at will, gives him the impression that the society is organized to satisfy his sexual wishes. When he is confronted by the hard reality of the bride-price, he discovers he cannot have a woman if he does not pay the money which he often does not have until his mid-twenties. If he wants to satisfy his sexual needs he must break the law and have illicit intercourse. He is likely to be very upset by sexual restrictions he was not told about early enough.

The unexpected frustration which society imposes on the sexual desires of a young man is allowed no outward expression. Aggression against the managers of the Moroccan economy, is violently discouraged and legally repressed. Anger towards the society turns in towards the family and the woman — object of his frustrated desire. The family offers the sexually and politically oppressed Moroccan male a natural outlet for his frustrations:

> A person who fears to express his aggression directly against the original social objects responsible for his frustration may express his aggression instead against some other objects . . . The tendency to express aggression against irrelevant objects would increase with increasing anxiety about expressing aggression against the actual source of frustration.[25]

A man who is both economically and sexually oppressed by his society is likely to find it less traumatizing to express his rage and resentment against his family than against his boss. And the society encourages him to do so. It encourages the male to perceive his honor primarily as maintaining an iron grip on his women and children. As Reich says, "sexual inhibition changes the structure of the economically oppressed in such a way that he acts, feels and thinks contrary to his own material interests."[26] The tragedy of the Moroccan youth who wants to love a woman is that his actions are likely to be directly opposed to his desires. The society's conditioning, starting with his relationship with his mother, and including the pressures on him to be "a real man," and his legal rights to subordinate his wife, is likely to produce reflexes which pertain more to hatred than love.

The traditional order, empowered by the codification of the Sharia into the modern *Code* of the family, views men and women as antagonists and dooms the conjugal unit to conflict. By affirming the man's right to have authority over women he can't control anymore, given the breakdown of traditional spatial and economic structures, the modern *Code* places the man in a humiliating situation where he perceives sexual desegregation and its effects as an emasculating phenomenon, given the difficulties he faces in fulfilling his traditional male role. For example, the rate of unemployment makes it difficult for the Moroccan male to perform the traditional duty of providing for his family. At the same time, allowing his wife to work outside under the supervision of other males makes him see himself, according to his traditional images of masculinity, as nothing more than a pimp (*kawwad*) or a cuckold (*karran*).

Male-female dynamics are influenced by two kinds of pressure:

1. The need, emerging from the process of desegregation, to value the heterosexual relationship and expect love and sex in the conjugal unit.
2. The pressures from the prevailing traditional patterns, symbolized by parental authority and enhanced by modern laws of the family to condemn the conjugal unit and debase sexual love.

The heterosexual relationship is caught between the poles of attraction and repulsion latent in traditional Muslim ideology. Modernization and economic necessity are breaking down the seclusion of women which was the traditional Muslim solution to the conflict. Sexual desegregation creates new tensions and anxieties. Space and authority boundaries between the sexes have become unclear, demanding confusing and painful adjustments from both men and women.

Women's Liberation in Muslim Countries

People tend to perceive women's liberation as a spiritual problem and not a material one. We have seen this to be true in the case of Islam where changes in conditions for women were perceived by Muslim male literature as being solely a religious problem. Muslims argued that changes in the woman's condition were a direct attack on Allah's realm and order. However, changes in woman's condition which took place in the twentieth century, mainly those which happened in socialist societies, showed that the liberation of women is predominantly an economic issue. Liberation is a costly affair for any society, and women's liberation is primarily a question of the allocation of resources. A society which decides to liberate women not only has to provide them with jobs, but also has to take upon itself the responsibility for providing child care and cooked food for all workers regardless of sex. A system of kindergartens and canteens is an indispensable investment to promote the liberation of women from traditional domestic chains.

The capacity to invest in women's liberation is not a function of the society's wealth, but of its goals and objectives. A society whose ultimate goal is profit rather than the development of human potential reveals itself to be reluctant and finally unable to afford a state system of child care centers and canteens. Marierosa Della Costa explains how capitalism maintains, in the midst of its modern management of human resources and services, a pre-capitalist army of wageless workers, the housewives, who provide unpaid-for child care and domestic services.[1] Hence the paradox: the "richest" nation in the world (that is the nation that succeeds in controlling most of the world's resources), the United States, is unable in spite of its much publicized abundance to afford a system of free kindergartens and canteens to promote women's humanhood. Meanwhile struggling and frugal China is trying to do so.[2] For Chinese communist society has decided to invest its profits in the human individual, rather than to invest the individual profit-making.

Third World countries, still in search of a path to development, have these two examples before them. Have Arab societies taken a stand on the question? Until now, they have had no effective systematic and coherent program. (Verbal wish-fulfillments excepted, of course, because they are neither effective nor systematic, although they may well be coherent, as is the case with Tunisia.) In the absence of such a program, and because it is too soon to judge the emerging trends in independent Arabo-Muslim states concerning the liberation of women, I will limit myself to a few speculative remarks on the likely future of women in the Arab world. Before going any further, I want to draw attention to the inadequacy of the only two models for "women's liberation" presently available in the Arabo-Muslim world.

The scarcity of effective models for "liberated women" could explain the particularly strong reaction that "women's liberation" evokes in most Muslims. (By effective I mean models which evoke specific images, specific enough to stir people's emotions.) One of these models is an intrinsic Arab model, that of pre-Islamic family and sexuality patterns (Jahiliya); the other is an exogenous model, the Western model. The socialist models of sexuality and family patterns are hardly known and enjoy a carefully cultivated indifference, based more often on ignorance than on a knowledgeable analysis. Both the pre-Islamic model and Western model provoke traumatizing images of sexuality, although for different reasons.

Pre-Islamic sexuality is described in Arab literature as a choatic, all-embracing, rampant promiscuity whose essence is the woman's self-determination, her freedom to choose and dismiss her sexual partner, or partners, and the utter unimportance of the physical father and paternal legitimacy. The idea of female sexual self-determination which is suggested by the terms "women's liberation" is likely to stir ancestral fears of this mythical Jahiliya woman (pre-civilized) in face of whom the male is deprived of all his initiative, control and privilege. The way to win over a "liberated woman" is to please her and make her love you, not to coerce her and threaten her. But Muslim society does not socialize men to win women through love; they are badly equipped to deal with a self-determined woman, whence the repulsion and fear which accompanies the idea of women's liberation.

Confusing sexual self-determination of women with chaotic lawless animalistic promiscuity is not exclusive to Muslim societies facing drastic changes in their family structure. This confusion existed and still exists in any society whose family system is based on the enslavement of the woman. Marx and Engels had to attack repeatedly the confusion of bourgeois writers which distorted their thinking about any family where the woman was not reduced to an aquiescent slave.[3] They had to show over and over that a non-bourgeois sexuality based on equality of the sexes does not necessarily lead to promiscuity, and consequently that the bourgeois family pattern was an unjustified dehumanization of half of society. The same argument holds equally for Muslim societies. Muslim marriage is based on the premise that social order can only be maintained if the woman's dangerous potential for chaos is restrained by a dominating non-loving husband who has besides his wife, other females (concubines, co-wives and prostitutes) available for his sexual pleasure under equally degrading conditions.[4] A new sexual order based on the absence of all dehumanizing limitations of the woman's potential means the destruction of the traditional Muslim family. In this respect, fears associated with changes in the family and the woman's condition are justified. These fears, embedded in the culture through centuries of women's oppression, are echoed and nourished by the vivid, fleshy, equally degrading images of Western sexuality and its disintegrating family patterns, portrayed on every imported television set.

It is understandable that Muslim fathers and husbands feel horrified at the idea of their own family and sexuality patterns being transformed into Western patterns. The striking characteristic of Western sexuality is the mutilation of the woman's integrity, her reduction to a few inches of nude flesh whose shades and forms are photographed *ad infinitum* with no goal other than profit. While Muslim exploitation of the female is clad under veils and buried behind walls, Western exploitation has the bad taste of being unclad, bare, and over-exposed.

It is worth noting that the fears of Muslim fathers and husbands are not totally unfounded; the nascent "liberation" of Muslim women has indeed borrowed many characteristics of Western women's way of life. The first gesture of "liberated" Arab women was to discard the veil for Western dress, which, in the thirties, forties and fifties, was that of the wife of the colonizer. Speaking a foreign language was often a corollary to discarding the veil, the first "liberated" women being usually members of the upper and middle classes. And here we touch upon another aspect of the difficulty present Muslim societies have in adjusting to female self-determination. The Westernization of the first "liberated" women was and still is part and parcel of the Westernization of the Arabo-Muslim ruling classes. The fears awakened by the Westernization of the women can be interpreted as simply another instance of Muslim society believing that males are able to select what is good in Western civilization and discard bad elements, while women are unable to choose correctly. This is concordant with the classical Muslim view of women as being unable to judge what is good and what is bad.

Another factor which helps in understanding men's fears of the changes taking place is that the Westernization of the women enhanced her seductive powers. We have seen that the Muslim ethic is against women's ornamenting themselves and exposing their charms; veil and walls were particularly effective anti-seduction devices. Westernization allowed ornamented and seductively clad female bodies to appear on the streets. It is interesting that while Western women's liberation movements had to repudiate the body in pornographic mass media, Muslim women are likely to claim the right to their bodies as part of their liberation movement. Previously a Muslim woman's body belonged to the man who possessed her, father or husband. The mushrooming of beauty salons and ready-to-wear boutiques in Moroccan towns can be interpreted as a forerunner of the woman's urge to claim her own body, which will culminate in more radical claims, such as the claim to birth control and abortion.

Having described the available models and their negative impact on the woman's question, I am going to hazard a few speculations on the future of women's liberation in Muslim societies, based on a projection from the current situation.

It is hardly contestable that there have been substantial changes in the Muslim women's condition. Women have gained many rights which were denied to them before, such as the right to education, the right to vote and be elected, and the right to use non-domestic spaces. But an important characteristic of this nascent ''liberation'' is that it is not the outcome of a careful plan of controlled nation-wide development as was the case in China. Neither is it the outcome of a massive involvement of women in labor markets, coupled with organized women's movements as was the case in the West. The partial, fragmented acquisition of rights by women in Arabo-Muslim countries is a random, non-planned, non-systematic phenomenon, due mainly to the disintegration of the traditional system under pressures from within and without. The Muslim women's liberation is likely therefore to follow a *sui-generis* pattern.

To the dismay of rigid conservatives desperately preoccupied with a static tradition, change is shaking the foundations of the Muslim world. Change is multidimensional and hard to control, especially for those who deny it. Accepted or rejected, change gnaws continuously at the intricate mechanisms of social life, and the more it is thwarted, the deeper and more surprising are its implications. The heterosexual unit is not yet officially admitted by Muslim rulers to be a crucial area in the process of national development. Development plans devote hundreds of pages to the mechanization of agriculture, mining, and banking, and only a few pages to the family and the women's condition. I want to emphasize on the one hand, the deep and far-reaching processes of change working in the Muslim family, and on the other hand, the decisive role of women and the family in any serious development plan in a Third World economy.

THE FAMILY AND THE WOMAN

As shown earlier, one of the distinctive characteristics of Muslim sexuality is its territoriality, which reflects a specific division of labor and a specific conception of society and of power. The territoriality of Muslim sexuality sets ranks, tasks, and authority patterns. Spatially confined, the woman was taken care of materially by the man who possessed her, in exchange for her total obedience and her sexual and reproductive services. The whole system was organized so that the Muslim *Umma* was actually a society of male citizens who possessed among other things the female half of the population. In his introduction to *The Woman and Socialism*, George Tarabishi remarks that people are saying that there are one hundred million Arabs, but in fact there are only fifty million, the female population being prevented from taking part in social responsibilities.[5] Muslim men have always had many more rights and privileges than Muslim women, including even the right to kill their women.(The Moroccan penal code still shows a trace of this power in article 418 which grants attenuating circumstances to a man who kills his adulterous wife.)[6] The man imposed on the women an artifically narrow existence, both physically and spiritually.

This territoriality (the confining of women) is in the process of being dismantled, modernization having triggered mechanisms of socio-economic change no group is able to control. Philip Slater, in his studies of societies built upon sex-antagonisms, came to the conclusion that such systems are only manageable "under conditions of strong ties and residential stability."[7] Morocco's family structure and tradition of residential stability is disintegrating with the increase of individual salaries and the breakdown of the corporate family system, at least in the group under study, the urban *petit bourgeoisie*. The majority of traditional women interviewed lived with their husbands' parents at the beginning of their married lives. Then, for "no reason," that is, with no open hostility, the extended family broke up. In two cases, the reason advanced was quarreling between son and uncle. But a century ago, quarrels did not break up Moroccan families. A more likely reason is the ability of the son to earn an adequate salary independent of his father and uncle. Having his own income, he is now able to break away. The fact that the state, the most important employer, requires from its civil servants a certain mobility is an important element in the destruction of the old family structure. Unnecessary confusion and anxiety stem from the fact that the government is supporting the traditional ideology and enforcing it as law, while its economic plans and programs promote a different reality. The new reality is shaking the traditional

103

structure, increasing role confusion and conflicts, and bringing increased suffering for the individuals involved, regardless of sex.

One of the results of the break-up of traditional family life is that, for the first time in the history of modern Morocco, the husband is facing his wife directly. Men and women live more closely and inter-act more than they ever did before, partly because of the absence of anti-heterosexual institutions such as the mother-in-law's presence and sexual segregation. This direct confrontation between men and women brought up in sexually antagonistic traditions is likely to be, in this transitional period, loaded with tensions and fears on both sides.

The future of male-female dynamics greatly depends on the way modern states handle the readjustment of sexual rights and the reassessment of sexual statuses. The Chinese regime, for example, renounced the medieval definitions of sex statuses and abolished what it termed the "feudal" marriage system. By the same token, China abolished the traditional division of labor within the family. In Morocco however the legislature retained the traditional concept of marriage. It reenacted, as the basis for family law, the ancient definition of sex statuses based on the division of labor according to sex: Article 35 defines the man as being sole provider for the family. He is responsible not only for himself but also for his able-bodied wife, who is consequently defined economically dependent, her participation being limited to sexual services, reproduction and housework.

To define masculinity as the capacity to earn a salary is to condemn men suffering from unemployment, or the threat of it, to perceive economic problems as threats of castration. Moreover, since the *Code* defines earning a salary as a man's role, a woman who earns a salary will be perceived as either masculine or castrating. If the privileges of men become more easily accessible to women, then men will be perceived as becoming more feminine.

By emphasizing the link between masculinity and economic success for men, the Moroccan *Code* reactivates traditional patterns of self-esteem whereby a man's prestige in the group depends on his wealth, and does so at the very moment when economic structure is making it difficult for a growing majority of Moroccans to amass wealth. The authority of males, traditionally embodied in their ability to provide for their families, is seriously jeopardized by the present situation. Moroccan males now have great difficulty achieving traditional masculine recognition:

> There is no power but in men
> There are no men without money.[8]

Modernization, in these terms, clearly appears to be a castrating phenomenon. By emphasizing the traditional definitions of masculinity, the state encourages ambivalent feelings in men, both towards the "inactive" women they cannot provide for and toward the "active" ones they experience as castrators. The ambivalence aggravates the traditional fears of devouring females latent in all patriarchal cultures. The Moroccan male is increasingly encouraged to look upon himself not as a multi-dimensional person, but primarily as a sexual agent, and it is from sex that he is encouraged to expect gratification, prestige and power. Moroccans ought to boss their wives and children, but if they dare to raise objections in economic and political situations, their initiatives are severely discouraged and often violently repressed. The complementarity between an authoritarian political structure and the authoritarian power of the husband and father seems to be a feature of transitional societies unable yet to create an effective development program and face change with effective planning. In Morocco, the events of the last decades have brought about a serious erosion of male supremacy which is generating increased tensions between the sexes, at least in this transitional period. Surprisingly enough, the serious blows to male supremacy did not come from the women who have been reduced by their historical situation to helplessness, but from the state.

THE STATE AS THE MAIN THREAT TO TRADITIONAL MALE SUPREMACY

In spite of its continuous support for traditional male rights, the state constitutes a threat and a mighty rival to the male as both father and husband. The state is taking over the traditional functions of the male head of the family, such as education and providing economic security for members of the household. By providing a nation-wide state school system, and an individual salary for working wives, daughters and sons, the state has destroyed two pillars of the father's authority. The increasingly preeminent role of the state has stripped the traditionally powerful head of the family of his privileges and placed him in a subordinate position *vis á vis* the state, not very different from the position of women *vis á vis* the traditional family. The head of the family is dependent on the state, the main employer, to provide for him, exactly as women are dependent on their husbands in traditional settings. Economic support is given in exchange for obedience, with the result of increasing male-female solidarity as a defense against the state and its daily frustrations.

The word "sexist" as it is currently employed in the American language has the connotation that males are favored at the expense of females by the established economic structure. It is my belief that, in spite of appearances, the

Muslim system does not favor men; the self-fulfillment of men is just as impaired and limited as that of women. Though this equality of the sexes' oppression is hidden in the midst of the world-renowned "privileges" of the Muslim male, I have tried to illustrate it by showing how polygamy and repudiation are oppressive devices for both sexes. The Muslim theory of sexuality views women as fatally attractive and the source of delights. Any restrictions on the man's right to such delights, even if they take the form of restrictions of the women only (seclusion, for example), are really attacks on the male's potential for sexual fulfillment.

It might well be argued that the Muslim system makes men pay a higher psychological price for the satisfaction of sexual needs than women, precisely because women are conditioned to accept sexual restrictions as a "natural" necessity while men are encouraged to expect a thorough satisfaction of their sexual needs. Men and women are socialized to deal with sexual frustration differently. We know that an individual's discontent grows as his expectations increase. From the age of four or earlier, a woman in Moroccan society is made aware of the sexual restrictions she has to face. The difficulties which a Moroccan male experiences in putting up with sexual frustration are almost unknown to the Moroccan woman who is traumatized early enough to build adequate defenses. In this sense also, the Muslim order is not "sexist."

FUTURE TRENDS

INCREASING MALE-FEMALE SOLIDARITY AND THE STRENGTHENING OF THE HETERO-SEXUAL UNIT

The reduced power of the head of the family is in the short run productive of tensions in the family where a resentful male is likely to compensate by oppressing his wife and child. But, in the long run, it is likely to generate increasing male-female rapprochement in the face of the common and increasingly similar preoccupations of their daily reality. It can lead, as it already has in the case of young couples, to an increased collaboration between husband and wife and a strengthening of the conjugal unit in the face of the system's short-comings.

We have seen that the only model for a conjugal unit available in a Muslim society dictates how men and women should relate. The relation in a traditional family is a master-slave relation where love is excluded and condemned as a weakness on the part of men. The separation between love and sex is clearly illustrated by another model of male-female relatedness, this time not taken from institutions, but from literature, the Udrite love model.[9] Udrite love is a trend of romantic love which constitutes a very important part of Arab litera-ture. It still enjoys endlessly renewed fame through the poems sung by the most famous Arab singers, broadcast by the mass media. The characteristic of the Udrite lover is that he never has sexual intercourse with his beloved, and because in Arabo-Muslim order marriage is synonymous with blessed sexual-ity, the Udrite lovers never marry. Countless obstacles from within and without stand between them forever, keeping their unsatisfied bodies burning with a "spiritual" flame. For centuries this love has been presented as the highest form of love where the soul triumphs over the flesh, the spirit over the body, refinement and sophistication over animality (spirit, soul, refinement and sophistication all being linked with the absence of sexual intercourse). The model of Udrite love is being attacked presently as a sick way of loving a woman. It is quite revealing that the most vicious attacks on Udrite love come from the male writers, Dr. Sadek Jalal al-Adm[10] and Tahar Labib Djedidi.[11] Both men, the first through a psycho-analytical approach and the second through a linguistic approach, come to similar conclusions. For Tahar Djedidi, Udrite love is the expression of an economically and politically impotent community, the Banu Udra, who were deprived of their traditional tribal privileges with the growth of the centralized Muslim Empire.[12] For Dr. Sadek Jalal al-Adm, Udrite love, which implies a man can only love a woman if he avoids sexual intercourse with her, is the distorted conception of love in a sexually oppressed society. Udrite love could only exist outside of the conjugal unit; the wife could never be the object of such love, by definition.

These recent analyses of Udrite love support my own conclusion, based on my analysis of the traditional conjugal models, that modern Muslim societies have to face the fact that the traditional family mutilates the woman by depriving her of her humanity. What modern Muslim societies ought to strive toward is a family based on the unfragmented wholeness of the woman. Sex with an unfragmented human female is a glorious act, not a soiling, degrading one. It implies and generates tenderness and love. Allegiance and involvement with an unfragmented woman do not take men away from their social duties because the woman is not a marginal tabooed individual; rather, she is the center, the source, the generator of order and life.

Islam's basically positive attitude towards sexuality is more conducive to healthy perspectives of a self-realizing sexuality, harmoniously integrated in the social life, than the West's basically negative attitudes toward sexuality. Serious changes in male-female conditioning in Western countries imply re-volutionary changes in the society which these reformist countries are deter-mined to avoid at any cost. Muslim societies *cannot* afford to be reformist; they do not have sufficient resources to be able to offer palliatives. A superficial replastering of the system is not a possible solution for them.

At a deeper level than laws and official policy, the Muslim social order views the female as a potent aggressive individual whose power can, if not tamed and curbed, corrode the social order. It is very likely that in the long run, such a view will facilitate women's integration into the networks of decision-making and power. One of the main obstacles Western women have been dealing with is their society's view of women as passive inferior beings. The fact that generations of university-educated women in both Europe and America failed to win access to decision-making posts in partly due to this deeply ingrained image of women as inferior. The Muslim image of women as a source of power is likely to make Muslim women set higher and broader goals than just equality with men. The most recent studies on the aspirations of both men and women seem to come to the same conclusion: the goal is not achieving equality with men. Women have seen that what men have is not worth getting. Women's goals are already being phrased in terms of a global rejection of established sexual patterns, frustrating for males and degrading for females. This implies a revolutionary reorganization of the entire society starting from its economic structure and ending with its grammar. Dr. Jalal al-Adm excuses himself at the beginning of his book for using the term "he" throughout the book while in fact he should be using a neutral term, because his findings are valid for both men and women.[13] As a social scientist he resents being a prisoner of the Arabic grammar which imposes on him a sex-defined pronoun.[14] But not many Arab males yet feel ill-at-ease with the sex-biased Arabic grammar, though a majority already feels indisposed by the economic situation.

The holders of power in Arab countries regardless of their political make-up are condemned to promote change, and they are aware of this fact, no matter how loud their claim to uphold the "prestigious past" as the path to modernity. Historians have interpreted the somewhat cyclical resurgence of traditional rhetoric as a reflex of ruling groups threatened by acute and deep processes of change.[15] The problem Arab societies face is not whether or not to change, but how fast to change. The link between women's liberation and economic development is evidenced by the similarities existing in conditions of the two sexes in the Third World; both sexes are suffering from exploitation and deprivation. Men do not have, as in the so-called "abundant" Western societies, glaring advantages over women. Illiteracy and unemployment are suffered by males as well as females. This similarity of men and women as equally deprived and exploited individuals assumes a huge importance in the likely evolution of Third world family structure. George Tarabishi pointed out the absurdity of men who argue that women should not be encouraged to get jobs in Arab society where men suffer from unemployment.[16] He argues that society should not waste human resources in unemployment, but systematically channel this wealth of resources into the productive tasks. The female half of human resources is more than welcome in the Arab future.

One could already speculate that women's liberation in an Arab context is likely to take a faster and a more radical path than in Western countries. Women in Western liberal democracies are organizing themselves to claim their rights, but their oppressors are strong, wealthy, and reformist regimes. The dialogue takes place within the reformist frame characteristic of the bougeois democracies. In such situations, serious changes are likely to take a long time. American women will get the right to abortion but it will be a long time before they can prevent the female's body from being exploited as a marketable product. Muslim women, on the contrary, engage in a silent but explosive dialogue with a fragil ruling class whose major task is to secure economic growth and plan a future without exploitation and deprivation. The Arab ruling class is beginning to realize that they are charged with building a sovereign future, which necessarily revolves around the location and adequate utilization of all human and natural resources for the benefit of the entire population. The Arab woman is a central element in any sovereign future. Those who have not realized this fact are misleading themselves and their country.

Changes in Employment Patterns
According to Sex and Area of Residence
(1960-1971)

Urban Areas	Total Population	Employed	Out of Work
1960			
Men	1,692,215	652,180	173,155
Women	1,719,456	147,458	5,445
1971			
Men	2,620,771	947,131	159,002
Women	2,736,392	240,581	56,656
Percent Increase			
Men		45%	−8%
Women		63%	939%
Rural Areas	Total Population	Employed	Out of Work
1960			
Men	4,116,957	1,959,037	124,240
Women	4,097,604	191,189	1,665
1971			
Men	4,965,134	2,152,184	117,046
Women	4,831,509	291,683	16,235
Percent Increase			
Men		10%	−6%
Women		53%	875%

Adapted from Tableau 1-8, *Recensement Generale de la Popuulation et de l'Habitat* (Royaume du Maroc: Secretariat d'Etat au Plan et au Developpement Regional, Direction de la Statistique, 1971) Vol. II, p. 30.

Notes

The version of the Quran used throughout this book is Mohammad Marmaduke Pickthall's *The Meaning of the Glorious Koran* (New York: New American Library, Mentor Religious Books, 13th printing, n.d.)

The abreviations used in the notes are:

B for *Bab* ("chapter")
H for *Hadith* ("verbal tradition of Mohammad")
K for *Kitab* ("book")
BESM for *Bulletin Economique et Social de Maroc*

NOTES TO PREFACE

It is interesting to note that this literature is mostly written by men. Muslim writers seem to perceive "the woman's problem" as a problem between the woman and Islam, as is illustrated by the following titles (my translations):

Sa'id al-Afghani, *Islam and the Woman,* 2nd ed. (Damascus: Dar al-Fikr, 1964).

'abd al-Kader al-Karamani, *The Woman from the Viewpoint of Islam* (Aleppo; Syria: al-Matba'a al-'ilmiya, n.d.).

Ja'far an-Naqdi, *Islam and the Woxuiativman,* 2nd ed. (Maktabat an-Najah).

Sadiq al-Kumayli, *The Woman's Personality in Islam* (Beirut, 1972).

Muhammad al-Shayyal, *The Woman in Islam* (Cairo: al-Matba'a as-Salafiya, n.d.).

Mahmud Shaltut, *The Woman and the Quran* (Cairo: Matba'at al-Azhar, 1963).

'abbas Mahmud al-Aqqad, *The Woman in the Quran* (Cairo: Dar-al-Hilal, n.d.).

'abd al-Qader al-Maghribi, *Muhammed and the Woman* (Beirut: al-Maktaba al-Ahliya, 1929).

Muhammad al-Mahdi al-Hajoui, *The Woman Between the Shar' and the Law* (Casablanca: Dar al-Kitab, 1967).

A. Afifi, *The Arab Woman in her Jahiliya and Her Islam* (Cairo: al-Maktaba at-Tijarya al-Kubra, n.d.).

Besides a general restating of the woman's position in Islam, the masculine literature on the woman focuses on another problem which seems to have been felt by men to be a central question:

Muhammad Nasr ad-Din al-Albani, *The Seclusion of the Muslim Woman in the Book and the Suna* (Beirut: al-Maktab al-Islami, n.d.).

Abu Radwan as-Sanusi, *The Woman Between Seclusion and De-seclusion* (Beirut: n.d.).

Abu al-A'la al-Mawdoodi, *Seclusion* (Damascus: Dar al-Fikr, n.d.).

Mustafa Naja, *Explanation of the Institution of Seclusion* (Beirut: al-Matba'a al-Wataniya, n.d.).

NOTES TO INTRODUCTION

1. *Code du Statut Personnel,* ("Code of Personal Status") Dahir #1-57-343, November 22, 1957. Bulletin Officiel #2378, May 23, 1958.
2. Ibn Anas Malik, *al-Muwatta* (Cairo: Mustafa al-Babi al-Halabi, n.d.).
3. Salama Musa, *The Woman is Not a Man's Toy* (Cairo: Salama Musa Li-nasr wa tawzi', 1955).
4. *Ibid.,* p. 53. See also Abdallah Laroui', *L'ideologie Arabe Contemporaine* (Paris: Francois Maspere, 1967), p. 51.
5. Salama Musa, *Woman is Not Man's Toy,* p. 106.
6. Kacem Amin, *Tahrir al-Mar'a ("The Liberation of the Woman"),* (Cairo: 'Umum al-Makatib Bismisr Wal-harij, the edition published on the occasion of the commemoration of the twentieth anniversary of the author's death, 1928), p. 18.
7. *Ibid.,* p. 15.
8. *Ibid.,* p. 16.
9. *Ibid.,* p. 10.
10. *Ibid.,* p. 9.
11. as-Salah Ibn Murad, *al-Hidad 'ala Mra-at al-Hadad,* 1st ed. (Tunis: al-Matba'a at-Tunusiya), p. 6.
12. *Ibid.,* p. 170.
13. Daniel Lerner, *The Passing of Traditional Society, Modernizing the Middle-East* (New York: MacMillan and Co., Free Press, 1958), p. 44.
14. *Ibid.,* p. 47.
15. Anouar Abdel-Malek, *Egypt, Military Society* (New York: Random House, Vintage Books, 1968), p. 249.
16. Paul Coatalen,. "Ethnologie Barbare" in *Annales Marocaines de Sociologie* (1970), pp. 3-11.
17. Allal al-Fasi, *The Independence Movements in Arab North Africa* (New York: Octagon Books, 1970), p. 381.
18. The first members of the Arab League were Egypt, Saudi Arabia, Iraq, Yemen, Syria, and Lebanon.
19. Allal al-Fasi, *Independence Movements in North Africa,* p. 409.

20. Wilfred Cantwell-Smith, *The Meaning and End of Religion,* (New York: New American Library, A Mentor Book, 1964), p. 79.
21. Montgomery Watt, *Muhammad at Medina* (Oxford: The Clarendon Press, 1956), p. 239.
22. H.A.R. Gigg, "Constitutional Organization" in *Origin and Development of Islamic Law,* ed. M. Khàduri and H. J. Liebesny, Vol. I (Washington, D.C.: Middle East Institute, 1955), p. 3.
23. Gertrude Stern, *Marriage in Early Islam* (London: The Royal Asiatic Society, 1931), p. 71.
24. Joseph Schacht, *An Introduction to Islamic Law* (London: Oxford University Press, 1964), p. 161.
25. In *The Muqaddimah, An Introduction to History* (translated from the Arabic by Franz Rosenthal, Princeton, N.J.: Princeton University Press, Bollingen Series, 1969). The North African historian Ibn Khaldun (1332-1406) sketched a model of the Muslim social order. He was interested in analyzing what was happening to the then disintegrating Muslim world, which had stood uncontested in the Mediterranean arena until a few centuries before. Although primarily concerned with an entirely different problem, the growth and death of civilization, Ibn Khaldun analyzed the reasons the Muslims had succeeded for so long.

    According to his theory, the survival of human groups requires the surrender of individual will to a set of social norms or laws. There are two kinds of social norms: those having a human basis, reason, and those having a supernatural basis, religion.

    > If these norms are ordained by the intelligent leading personalities and minds of the dynasty, the result will be a political [institution] with an intellectual [rational] basis, if they are ordained by God through a lawgiver who establishes them as [religious] laws, the result will be a political [institution] with a religious basis. (Ibn Khaldun, *The Muqaddimah,* p. 154).

    A political institution having a religious basis is far superior to a political institution having a rational basis, not because of any deficiency in the latter's mechanisms, but because of the narrowness of its scope. Reason governs only this world's interests while religious institutions govern both:

    > Political laws consider only worldly interests. On the other hand, the intention the lawgiver has concerning mankind is their welfare in the other world, therefore it is necessary, as required by the religious law, to cause the mass to act in accordance with the religious laws in all their affairs touching both this world and the other world. (Ibn Khaldun, *The Muqaddimah,* p. 155).

26. H. A. R. Gibb, "Constitutional Organization," p. 3.
27. S. G. Vesey-Fitzgerald, "Nature and Source of the *Sharia*" in *Origin and Development of Islamic Law,* p. 109.
28. *Ibid.,* p. 104.
29. *Ibid.,* p. 85.
30. J. Schacht, *Introduction to Islamic Law,* p. 76.
31. *Ibid., p. 101.*
32. *Ibid.,* pp. 210-214.
33. *Ibid.,* p. 100.
34. Abdallah Laroui, *L'Historie du Maghreb, Un Essai de Synthese* (Paris: Maspero, 1970) p. 346.
35. This opportunism is clearly illustrated in the economic options adopted by the Moroccan State during the 17 years of independence. A revealing analysis of these options is Samir Amin's *Le Maghreb Modern* (Paris: Editions de Minuit, 1970) Chapter VI: "Le Maroc, Hesitations et Contradictions." Also A. Belal, "L'Orientation des Investissements et les Imperatifs du Developpement National," *Bulletin Economique et Social du Maroc* (hereinafter referred to as *BESM*) XXVIII, p. 100; and T. Ben Cheikh's, "Planification et Politique Agricole," Part I *BESM* XXXI, No. 112-113 (January-June 1969) pp. 191, 199, and Part II in *BESM,*

(July-September 1969) No. 114, XXXI, pp. 75-83.
36. Salama Musa, *Woman Is Not Man's Ivy*, chapter entitled "Our Philosophy Concerning the Woman," p. 85.
37. Dahir N° I-57-190, August 19, 1957, Published in *Le Bulletin Officiel*, N° 2341, September 6, 1957, p. 1163.
38. There are four schools of law among Orthodox Muslims:
    The Hanafees: Mainly in Central Asia, Northern India, and among the Turks (but also in Pakaistan, China and Japan). The founder of the school is Abu Hanifa (699-769), the father of the deductive method which undertook to create precedents in Muslim law by analogy with other laws and according to the decisions of the first four caliphs.
    The Shafees: Mainly in Lower Egypt, Southern India, and in Malaya. The founder is Abu Abdallah Muhammad Ash-Shafe'e (770-819). He laid special stress upon the methodological investigation of the foundation of the Law.
    The Malekites: Mainly in North Africa and Upper Egypt. The founder is Malik Ibn Anas (705-795). Malik confined his teaching to the traditions. The title of his main work, *al-Muwatta,* means "the path," a synonym of the *Sunna,* Malik's school is the most closest to the traditions.
    The Hanbalees: Mainly in Central and Eastern Arabia. The founder is Abu Hanifa (780-855). The school is characterized by a puritanical tendency which aims at restoring the original purity of religious observance.
    The four schools are in agreement in regards to the fundamental dogmas "though they differ from each other in the application of private judgement, and in the interpretation and exposition of the Quran."
38. Ibn Anas Mallik, *al-Muwatta,* (Cario: Mustafa al-Halabi, nd.).

NOTES TO CHAPTER 1

1. Ibn Khaldun, *The Muqaddimah, An Introduction to History,* translated by Franz Rosenthal (Princeton, N.J.: Princeton University Press, Bollingen Series, 1969) pp. 160-161.
2. *Ibid.,* p. 161
3. *Ibid.*
4. Abu-Hamid al-Ghazali, *Ihya Ulum ad-Din, ("The Revivification of Religious Sciences")* (Cairo: al-Maktaba at Tijariya al-Kubra, n.d.).
5. *Ibid.,* p. 28.
6. *Ibid.,* p. 25.
7. *Ibid.,* p. 25.
8. *Ibid.,* p. 27.
9. George Peter Murdock, *Social Structure* (New York: MacMillan & Co. Free Press), 1965, p. 273.
10. *Ibid.*
11. Kacem Amin, *The Liberation of the Woman,* (Cairo: 'Umum al-Makatib Bimisr Wa-Iharij, 1928) p. 64.
12. *Ibid.,* p. 65.
13. al-Ghazali, *The Revivification of Religious Sciences,* Vol. II, chapter on marriage; and Mizan al-'Amal ("Criteria for Action") (Cairo: Dar al-Ma'arif, 1964).
14. 'Abbas Mahmud al-Aqquad, *The Women in the Koran* (Cairo: Dar al-Hilal, n.d.).
15. *Ibid.,* p. 7; the verse he refers to is verse 228 of Surah II which is striking by its inconsistency. The whole verse reads as follows:
    And they [women] have rights similar to those [of men] over them in kindness, and men are a degree above them.
    tempted to interpret the first part of the sentence as a simple stylistic device to bring out the hierarchical content of the second part.

translation of the Quran used throughout is that of Mohammed Marmaduke Pickthall, *The Meaning of the Glorious Koran,* (New York: New American Library, A Mentor Religious Book, 13th printing, n.d.)

16. *Ibid.,* p. 24.
17. *Ibid.,* p. 25. The biological assumptions behind Aqquad's sweeping generalizations are obviously fallacious.
18. *Ibid.,* p. 18.
19. *Ibid.,* p. 26.
20. A. Schutz, "The Problem of Social Reality" *Collected Papers,* Vol. I (The Hague: Martinus Nijhoff, n.d.) p. 101
21. Ralph Linton, *The Study of Man,* (London: Appleton-Century Co., 1936), p.116.
22. A Schultz, *Collected Papers,* p. 9.
23. Sigmund Freud, *New Introductory Lectures on Psychoanalysis,* College Edition, (New York: Norton and Co., 1965), p. 114.
24. *Ibid.*
25. Sigmund Freud, *Three Contributions to the Theory of Sex,* 2nd ed. (New York: Dutton and Co., 1909) p. 77.
26. Sigmund Freud, *New Introductory Lectures,* p. 114.
27. al-Ghazali, *Revivification of Religious Sciences,* p. 51.
28. Una Stannard, "Adam's Rib or the Woman Within," *Transaction,* November-December 1970, Vol. 8, Special Issue on the American Woman, pp. 24-36.
29. al-Ghazali, *Revivification,* p. 50. Not only is the woman granted ejaculation, she is also granted the capacity to have nocturnal ejaculation and "sees what the man sees in sleep." (Ibn Saad, *Kitab at-Tabaqat Al Kubra,* Dar Beyrouth 1958). (Beirut: Vol. 8, "On Women" p. 858.)
30. Sigmund Freud, *Sexuality and the Psychology of Love* (New York: Collier Books, 1963 pp. 196-197.
31. *Ibid.,* p. 190.
32. Sigmund Freud, *Three Contributions,* p. 78.
33. *Ibid.*
34. *Ibid.*
35. Sigmund Freud, *New Introductory Lectures,* p. 132.
36. al-Ghazali, *Revivification,* p. 50.
37. *Ibid.*
38. *Ibid.*
39. Sigmund Freud, *Three Contributions,* p. 14.
40. *Ibid.,* p. 15.
41. al-Ghazali, *Revivification,* p. 50.
42. *Ibid.*
43. Sigmund Freud, *New Introductory Lectures,* p. 116.
44. Abbi 'Issa at-Tarmidi, *Sunan at-Tarmidi* (Medina: al-Maktaba as Salafiya, n.d.) Vol. II, p. 413, Bab: 9, Hadith: 1167. (Hereinafter Bab will be indicated by the letter B, and Hadith by the letter H.)
45. Abu al-Hassan Muslim, *al-Jami' as-Sahih* (Beirut: al-Maktaba at-Tijariya, n.d.) Vol. III, Book of Marriage, p. 130.
46. at-Tarmidi, *Sunan at-Tramidi,* p. 419, B:16, H:1181. See also al-Bukhari, *Kitab al-Jami' as-Sahih* (Leyden, Holland: Ludolph Krehl, 1868) Vol. III, Kitab 67, B:11. (Hereinafter Kitab will be indicated by the letter K.)
47. at-Tarmidi, *Sunan at-Tarmidi,* p. 419, B:17, H:1172.
48. Edward Westermarck, *The Belief in Spirits in Morocco,* (Abo, Finland: Abo-Akademi, 1920).
49. Edward Westermarck, *Wit and Wisdom in Morocco: A Study of Native Proverbs* (London: MacMillan and Co., 1926) p. 330.

50. Sidi Abderahaman al-Majdoub, *Les Quatrains du Mejdoub le Sarcastique, Poete Maghrebin du XVIieme Siecle,* collected and translated by J. Scelles-Millie and B. Khelifa (Paris: G. P. Maisonneuver and Larose, 1966) p. 161.
51. *Ibid.,* p. 160.
52. Abu Abd Allah Muhammad Ibn Ismail al-Bukhari, *Kitab al-Jami' as-Sahih* (Leyden, Holland: Ludolph Krehl, 1868) p. 419, K:67, B:18.
53. al-Ghazali, *Revivification,* p. 28.
54. Sigmund Freud, *Civilization and Its Discontents* (New York: Norton and Co., Inc., 1962).
55. Sigmund Freud, *A General Introduction to Psychoanalysis* (New York: Pocket Books, 1952) p. 27.
56. al-Ghazali, *Revivification,* p. 32.

NOTES TO CHAPTER 2

1. Ignaz Goldziher, *Muslim Studies,* (Chicago: Aldine Publishing Co., 1967) "What is Meant by Al-Jahiliya," p. 201.
2. Abu Abd Allah Muhammad Ibn Ismail al-Bukhari, *Kitab al-Jami' as-Sahih* (Leyden, Holland: Ludolph Krehl, 1868) p. 428, K: 67, B: 31.
3. In *at-Hayat al-Jinsiya, Inda al-Arab ("The Sexual Life of the Arabs")* (Beirut: Dar al-Kitab al-Jadid, 1958) Dr. Salah ad-Din al-Munajid tries to show that Islam did not impose any restrictions on the sexual indulgence which prevailed during the *Jahiliya.* According to him Islam only codified and regularized the previous sexual practices. It seems obvious to me that Dr. al-Munajid must be thinking of male sexuality only.
4. Abu-Hamid al-Ghazali, *The Revivification of Religious Sciences* (Cario: al-Maktaba at-Tijariya al-Kubra, n.d.) p. 30.
5. Edvard Westermark, *Wit and Wisdom in Morocco, A Study of Native Proverbs* (London: G. Routledge and Sons, Ltd., 1930) p. 329.
6. al-Ghazali, *Revivification*, p. 30.
7. *Ibid.*
8. Quran Surah II: 231
9. al-Bukhari, *al-Jami as-Sahih,* p. 426, K: 67, B: 35.
10. Ibn Hisham ed., *Sirat an-Nabi,* written by Ibn Ishaq, (Cairo: Matba'at al-Madani, 1963) p. 121.
11. Ibn Saad, *Kitab at-Tabaqat al-Kubra,* vol. 8, "On Women" (Beirut: Dar Beyrouth Lit-tiba'a wan-nasr, 1958) pp. 154 and 150.
12. *Ibid.,* p. 150.
13. *Ibid.,* p. 201.
14. *Ibid.,* p. 141.
15. *Ibid.,* p. 145.
16. *Ibid.,* p. 141 and p. 148.
17. *Ibid.,* p. 145.
18. al-Bukhari, *al Jami' as-sahih,* p. 459, K: 68, B: 3.
19. Ibn Saad, *at-tabaqat,* pp. 145, 148.
20. al-Bukhari, *Al Jami' as-sahih,* p. 459, K: 68, B: 3.
21. Abu Issa at-Tarmidi, *Sunan at-Tarmidi* (Medina: al-Maktaba as-Salifiya, nd.) p. 275, B: 4, H: 1092.
22. Ibn Saad, *at-Tabaqat,* pp. 120-123.
23. *Ibid.,* p. 129.
24. *Ibid.,* p. 212.
25. *Ibid.,* p. 213.
26. Quran, Surah: LXVI: 3.
27. Ibn Saad, *at-tabqat,* p. 212.

28. *Ibid.,* p. 117.
29. *Ibid.*
30. *Ibid.,* p. 153.
31. *Ibid.,* p. 101.
32. Quran, Surah XXXIII: 37.
33. at-Tarmidi, *Sunan at-tarmidi,* p. 404, B: 40, H: 1149. See also al-Ghazali, *Revivification,* p. 48. On the Prophet's involvement with his youngest wife, Aicha, see Nabia Abbot's *Aicha, the Beloved of Muhammad,* (Chicago: University of Chicago Press, 1942).
34. Robert Roberts, *The Social Laws of the Quran,* (London: Williams and Norgate, 1952) p. 13.
35. J. Schact, *Introduction to Islamic Law,* p. 125; also Malik, *al-Mawatta,* p. 11.
    In Muhammad's time the punishment was immurement:
    > As for those of your women who are guilty of lewdness, call to witness four of you against them. And if they testify [to the truth of the allegation] then confine them to the house until death takes them or [until] Allah appoint for them a way [through new legislation]. (Quran, Surah IV: 15)

    A new Muslim Law was revealed in Surah XXIV: 2-10 which changed the punishment to scourging:
    > The adulterer and the adulteress scourge each one of them a hundred stripes.
36. *Encyclopedia of Islam,* first edition, (Leyden, Holland: E. J. Brill, Ltd, 1934 S. V. *"zina."*
37. Quran, Surah LX: 12.
    It is important to understand the consensus under which women swore allegiance to Islam. Hind Bint Utba, an aristocratic Meccan woman, is reported to have reacted thus,
    > The Prophet: And you will not commit *zina?*
    > Hind: And does a free woman commit *zina?*
    > The Prophet: And you will not kill your children? [a reference to female infanticide]
    > Hind: And did you spare the life of any of our children? You killed all of them yourself at Badr. [a reference to the Battle of Badr, where the Muslims attacked Muhammed's own tribe] (Ibn Saad, *at-Tabaqat,* p. 9).

    Hind's answer concerning *zina,* although startling, is quite enigmatic. It can mean either that Hind thought that *zina* was a debasing act which she, as a noble woman, would not engage in, or it could mean, on the contrary, that Hind thought that, as a freeborn woman, no sexual union she engaged in could be debasing. The Muslim interpretation would be the first one.

    Gertrude Stern inclines toward the second possibility. [*Marriage in Early Islam,* (London: The Royal Asiatic Institute, 1939) p. 9.]

    Hind does not seem to be a particularly zealous Muslim who was ready to accept the new creed unconditionally and uncritically. Her opinion about the Prophet seems to be critical, as her answer concerning the killing of children shows. She contested the Prophet's right to ask her not to kill her unwanted babies because, as the leader of the Muslims, he had made war on his own tribe and so in effect killed his own relatives.
38. Quran, Surah XXIV: 32; also al-Bukhari, *al-Jami' as-Sahih,* pp. 410-411, K: 67, B: 1, 2, 3,; also Muslim, *al Jami as-Sahih,* pp. 128, 129, 130; and finally al-Ghazali, *Revivification,* pp. 22.
39. Gertrude Stern, *Marriage in Early Islam,* (London: The Royal Asiatic Society, 1939) p. 94.
40. al-Bukhari, *al Jami' as-Sahih,* p. 445, K: 67, B: 85.
41. Quran, Surah II: 222.
42. al-Ghazali, *Revivification,* p. 50.
43. Malik, *al-Muwatta,* p. 33.
44. Article 154, *Code du Statut Personnel.*
45. Malik, *al-Mawatta,* p. 19. Also Quran, Surah IV: 34; and al-Bukhari, *al-Jami as-Sahih,* p. 447, K: 67, B: 93.
46. Malik, *al-Muwatta,* p. 19.

47. *Ibid.*
48. Article 152, *Code du Statut Personnel.*
49. Malik, *al-Muwatta,* p. 23.
50. J. Schacht, *Islamic Law,* p. 164.
51. Malik, *al-Muwatta,* p. 23.
52. Montgomery Watt, *Muhammad at Mdina* (London: Oxford University Press, 1956) pp. 273-274. Also Excursust J, p. 373.
53. at-Tarmidi, *Sunan at-Tarmidi* p. 339, B: 33, H: 1140.
54. Quran, Surah LXV: 4.
55. Quran, Surah II: 226, 228, 234.
56. Quran, Surah LXV: 4.
57. Malik, *al-Muwatta,* p. 30.

NOTES TO CHAPTER 3

1. Ibn Saad, *Kitab at-Tabaqat al-Kubra,* Vol. 8 (Beirut: Dar Beyreuth, 1958).
2. Gertrude Stern, *Marriage in Early Islam* (London: The Royal Asiatic Society, 1939).
3. *Ibid.,* p. 70.
4. *Ibid.,* p. 73.
5. *Ibid.*
6. *Ibid.,* p. 62.
7. *Ibid.,* p. 66.
8. Ibn Hisham, ed., *Sirat an-Nabi,* written by Ibn Ishaq (Cairo: Matba'at al-Madani, 1963), Vol. I, p. 89. Also Ibn Saad, *at-Tabaqat,* Vol. I, p. 79.
9. Ibn Hisham, *Sirat,* p. 89.
10. Ibn Saad, *At-tabaqat,* Vol. 8, p. 95.
11. *Ibid.,* pp. 100, 118.
12. al-Bukhari, *al-Jami as-Sahih,* p. 453, K:67, B:109.
13. Ibn Saad, *al-Tabaqat,* p. 337.
14. *Ibid.,* p. 130.
15. Abu-al-Faraj al-Isbahani, *Kitab al-Aghani* (Beirut: Dar at-Taqafa, 1909) Vol. XVI, p. 102.
16. *Ibid.,* p. 93.
17. Sir John Glubb, *A Short History of the Arab Peoples* (New York: Stein and Day Publishers, 1970), p. 43.
18. Muhammad Ibn-Habib al-Bagdadi, *Kitab al-Muhabbar* (Hyderabad: 1942).
19. The translation is that of A.F.L. Beetson in his article, "The So-Called Harlots of Hadramaout," *Oriens* V, 1952, p. 16.
20. *Ibid.,* p. 18.
21. *Ibid.,* p. 20.
22. *Ibid.*
23. W. Robertson Smith, *Kinship and Marriage in Early Arabia* (Boston: Beacon Press, 1903), p. 94.
24. *Ibid.,* p. 92.
25. *Ibid.,* p. 156.
26. *Ibid.,* p. 172.
27. *Ibid.,* p. 92.
28. *Ibid.,* p. 121.
29. al-Isfahini, *Al Agani.* Translation by W. R. Smith in *Kinship in Early Arabia,* p. 80.
30. al-Isfahini, *Al Agani,* Vol. 16, p. 80.
31. al-Bukhari, *al-Tami as-Sahih,* p. 428, K:67, B:36. The translation is from M. Watt's *Muhammad at Medina* (London: Oxford University Press, 1956), pp. 378-379.

32. *Ibid.*, p. 423, K:67, B:31.
33. Tarmidi, *Sunan at-Tarmidi*, p. 395, B:27, H:1130.
34. Muslim, *al-Tami' as-Sahib*, pp. 130-131.
35. The Muslim world is divided into two camps: the sunnites and the sh'ites. The sunnites, or orthodox, are so called because they follow the *sunna*, traditions having authority concurrent to and supplementary with the Quran. The shi'ites are the partisans of the house of Ali, Mohammad's disciple, cousin, and son-in-law. They reject the authority of the *sunna* and they believe that the sovereign Imamat (''the leadership of the faithful'') is vested in Ali and his.descendants, the sons of his wife (the Prophet's daughter) Fatima. Consequently, they regard the first three caliphs, Abu Bakr, Omar and Othman, as usurpers. They are found chiefly in Persia (Iran) and India but their influence has penetrated into other parts of the Muslim world.
36. W. R. Smith, *Kinship in Early Arabia*, p. 85.
37. *Ibid.*, p. 94.
38. On the controversy concerning what constitutes the basic family unit, the trio mother-father-child or the duo mother-child, see the dialogue between R. Briffault and B. Malinowski in *Marriage, Past and Present* (Boston: Porter Sargent Publisher, 1956), Chapter III: ''What is a Family?''. A humorous summary of the controversy is Robin Fox's *Kinship and Marriage* (New York: Pelican Books, 1967), Chapter I: ''Kinship, Family and Descent.''
39. W. R. Smith, *Kinship in Early Arabia*, p. 177.
40. *Ibid.*, p. 38.
41. Salama Musa, *The Woman is Not a Man's Toy* (Cairo: Salama Musa Li-Nazr wa Tawzi, 1955), p. 20.
42. W. R. Smith, *Kinship in Early Arabia*, chapters II, IV and V.
43. A. R. Radcliffe-Brown and Daryll Forde, *African Systems of Kinship and Marriage* (London: International African Institute, Oxford University Press, 1950), p. 43.
44. M. Watt, *Muhammad at Medina*; Montgomery Watt, *Muhammad at Mecca* (London: Oxford University Press, 1953).
45. M. Watt, *Muhammad at Medina*, p. 290.
46. *Ibid.*, p. 261.
47. *Ibid.*, p. 290 and p. 388.
48. This argument is a clicheised by traditionists and modernists alike. Kacem Amin argues in this sense when defending the position Islam granted the women. A typical case of the use of the cliche is that of Muhammad al-Mahdi al-Hajoui in his book, *al-Mar'a Bayna as-Shar' wal-qanun* (Casablanca: Dar al-Kitab, n.d.).
49. Edouard Fares, *L'Honneur Chez Les Arabes Avant L'Islam: Etude de sociologie* (Paris: Adrien-Maisonneuve, 1932), p. 79.
50. M. Watt, *Muhammad at Medina*, p. 276.
51. Muhammad Marmaduke Pickthall, *The Meaning of the Glorious Koran* (New York: New American Library, a Mentor Religious Classic, n.d.), Introduction, p. 79.
52. M. Watt, *Muhammad at Medina*, p. 265.
53. *Ibid.*, p. 145.
54. *Ibid.*, p. 301.
55. *Ibid.*, p. 273.
56. *Ibid.*, p. 271.
57. al-Bukhari, *al-Jami as-Sahih*, p. 440, K: 67, B: 81; also p. 447, K: 67, B: 90.

NOTES TO CHAPTER 5

1. P. Pascon and M. Bentahar, ''Ce que disent 269 Jeunes Ruraux,'' *Bulletin Economique at Social du Maroc* (hereinafter referred to by the initials *BESM*), January- June 1969, XXI no. 112-113.

2. *Ibid.*, p. 75.
3. *Population Legale,* (Royaume du Maroc: Division des Statistiques, 0000) p. XII.
4. *Recensement Generale de la Population et de la Habitat* (Royaume du Maroc: Secretariat d'Etat au Plan et au Developpement Regional, Direction de la Statistique, 1971) vol. 1, p. 5.
5. Parcon and Bentahar, "269 Jeunes Ruraux," p. 63.
6. *Ibid.*, p. 76.
7. *Ibid.*
9. Abdeljalil Agouram and Abdelaziz Belal, "Bilan de l'Economie Marocaine Depuis l'Independence," *BESM* XXXIII no. 116, p. 11.
10. *Recensement Generale,* 1971, vol. 1, p. 9.
11. Pascon and Bentahar, "269 Jeunes Ruraux," p. 75.
12. Malika Belghiti, "Les Relations Feminines Et Le Statut De La Femme Dans la Famille Rurale," *Collection du Bulletin Economique Et. Social du Maroc,* (Rabat: 1970) p. 24.
13. "Enquete d'Opinion Sur la Planification Familiale en Milieu Urbain," (Royaume du Maroc: Division Des Statistiques, Ministere de la Sante Publique, 1966) p. 12.
14. *'Ahd* is a binding verbal promise. Edvard Westermark gives a description of the *'Ahd* mechanism in *Ritual and Belief in Morocco,* Vol. I (London: Macmillan and Co., 1926), p. 564.
15. The Quran considers the sexual relationship between son-in-law and mother-in-law incestuous: Suran IV: 23.
16. A basic description of the mechanism of the parent's curse is in E. Westarmark, *Wit and Wisdom* (London: George Routledge and Sons, 1930).

NOTES TO CHAPTER 6

1. al-Ghazali, *Revivification of Religious Sciences* (Cairo: al-Maktaba at-Tijariya al-Kubra, n.d.) p.39.
2. *Ibid.*
3. Quran, Suran 78: 32.
4. Revulsion with sex itself is, of course, an idea alien to orthodox Islam. Ghazali is supposed to have written *The Revivification* during a mystical ascentic retreat between 1095 and 1105 A.C.
5. al-Ghazali, *Mizan Al-Amal* "Criterion for Action" (Cairo: Dar al-Maarif, 1964) p. 317.
6. E. Westermark, *Wit and Wisdom in Morocco,* (London: George Routledge and Sons, 1930) p. 329. The first two proverbs can be traced to the second Caliph, Omar Ibn al-Khattab. See al-Ghazali's *Revivification*, p. 44.
7. Quran, Surah IV: 34. See remarks on the subject of beating in al-Ghazali, *Revivification,* p. 49; J. Schacht, *Introduction to Islamic Law,* p. 166; and Y. Linant De Bellefonds, *Traite De Droit Musulman Compare* (The Hague: Mouton and Co., and Paris: Maison des Sciences de l'Homme, 1965) p. 294.
8. al-Bukhari, *al-Jami' as-Sahih* p. 448, K: 67, B: 93; Tarmidi, *Sunan at-Tarmidi* p. 415, B: 11, H: 1173.
9. Article 56, *Code du Statut Personnel.*
10. *Dahsousa* is a symbolic nuptual tent made of drapes arranged within the nuptual room to emphasize the privacy of the married couple in the usually overcrowded house where the marriage takes place.
11. al-Ghazali, *Rivivification* p. 56.
12. Quran, Surah IV: 43.
13. al-Ghazali, *Revivification,* p. 28.
14. *Ibid.*, p. 50.
15. *Ibid.*, p. 49.

16. Sandor Ferenczi, *Thalassa, A Theory of Genitality* (New York: Norton and Co., 1968) p. 17.

17. al-Ghazali, *Revivification* p. 50. The verse is from the Quran, Surah 25: 54. Other reports on the words a Muslim is supposed to pronounce during coitus are in Imam Buhari, *al-Jami' as-Sahih* p. 439, K: 67, B: 66; and Imam Tarmidi, *Sunan at-Tarmidi*, p. 277, B: 8, H: 1098.

18. Max Weber, "Religious Rejections of the World and Their Directions," in *From Max Weber* translated by H. Gerth and C. Wright Mills (New York: Oxford University Press, Galaxy Books, 1958) p. 347.

19. Quran, Surah II: 165.

20. Quran, Surah III: 4.

21. On God's jealousy, see Imam Bukhari, *al-Jami' as-Sahih*, p. 451, K: 67, B: 107, 106; and Imam Tarmidi, *Sunan Al-Tarmidi*, p. 417, B: 14, H: 1178.

22. E. Westermark, *Wit and Wisdom*, p. 329.

24. W. Stephens, *The Oedipus Complex, Cross Cultural Evidence,* (New York: Free Press of Glencoe, 1962) p. 6.

25. The master of a concubine can choose to limit her to a domestic function or to raise her to the status of lover with privileges including the legitimacy of her children and their right to inherit.

26. The *Hajr:* if a man is not attracted anymore by a concubine, he can refuse interaction with her, even at the verbal level, and her dismissal often reflects on the children's position within the harem community. The female object of *hajr* loses her status and her rights as favorite, as lover, and she is often looked down upon by her fellow wives and concubines. Often she is associated with "bad luck" and evil eye.

27. The rate of Morocco in 1952 was already very small — 6.6%. It has probably decreased since then. See William Goode, *World Revolution and Family Patterns* (New York: Glencoe Press, 1963) p. 103; also R. Patai, *Society, Culture and Change in the Middle East* (Philadelphia: University of Pennsylvania Press, 1962) pp. 92-93.

28. al-Ghazali, *Revivification* p. 48.

29. Ibn Saad, *at-tabaqat,* Vol. 8, p. 192; see also al-Bukhari, *al-jami' as-Sahih* p. 412, K: 67, B: 4.

30. D. J. L. Roland, "Development de la Personnalite et Incidences de l'Environment Au Maroc, " *Maroc Medical,* December 1964, pp. 269-272.

31. M. Achour, "Vue particuliere du Probleme de l'environnement en fonction du milieu scolaire marocain," *Maroc Medical,* December 1964, p. 329.

NOTES TO CHAPTER 7

1. The link between the child's experience with his mother and his capacity to relate to a person of the other sex is the crux of the Freudian concept of "Oedipus Complex."

2. P. Slater, *The Glory of Hera* (Boston: Beacon Press, 1968), p. 414.

3. Quran, Surah XLVI: 15.

4. Quran, Surah IV: 1, Surah XXXI: 14, Surah VI: 152, Surah XVII: 23, Surah XXIX: 8.

5. Sigmund Freud, "The Most Prevalent Form of Degradation of Erotic Life," in *Sexuality and the Psychology of Love* (New York: Collier Books, MacMillan Publishing, 1970).

6. Dorothy Blisten, *The World of the Family* (New York: Random House, 1963), pp. 204-205.

7. Sidi Abderahaman al-Majdoub, in *Les quatrains du Mejdoub le Sarcastique, Poete Maghrebin du XVIeme siecle,* collected and translated by J. Scelles-Millie and B. Khelifa (Paris: Maisonneuve & Larose, 1966), p. 180.

8. E. Westermark, *Wit and Wisdom* (London: George Routledge and Sons, 1930), p. 326.

9. al-Majdoub, *Les Quatrains du Mejdoub,* p. 180.

10. P. Slater, *The Glory of Hera,* p. 30.

11. Article 36, *Code du Statut Personnel.* E. Goffman points out the tactical importance of deference rules in authoritarian relationships in *Asylums* (New York: Anchor Books, Doubleday and Co., 1961), p. 115.

12. E. Goffman, *Asylums,* p. 41.

NOTES TO CHAPTER 8

1. The term "territoriality," however, is too primitive really for the phenomenon we want to understand, which is a sophisticated, manifold use of space. Hall's concept of "proxemics" is more suitable:

   > Proxemics is the term I have coined for the interrelated observations and theories of man's use of space and a specialized elaboration of culture. [Edward Hall, *The Hidden Dimension (New York: Doubleday, Anchor Books, 1969), p. 1*]

   According to Hall, the dangers are great, given the sensuous dimension of any physical interaction, of involving the individuals in an atmosphere of ambiguous signs, unconsciously sent and received:

   > Man's sense of space is closely related to his sense of self, which is in an intimate transaction with his environment. Man can be viewed as having visual, kinesthetic, tactile, and thermal aspects of his self which may be either inhibited or encouraged to develop by his environment. [E. Hall, *The Hidden Dimension,* p. 63]

2. In *Purity and Danger* (Baltimore: Pelican Books, 1970) Mary Douglas emphasized the links in social structure between the concept of boundaries, the concept of danger, and the concept of power.
3. *Ibid.,* p. 14.
4. Women are considered in Moroccan folklore to be the depository of devilish forces: Edmund Doutte, *Magie et Religion Dans l'Afrique du Nord* (Algiers: Societe Musulmane du Maghreb, 1908), p. 33; also, E. Westermark, *The Belief in Spirit in Morocco* (Abo: Abo Akadem, 1920), p. 22. The Moroccan psychologist Abdelwanad Radi in "Processus de Socialization de l'Enfant Morocain," *Etudes Philosophiques et Litteraires,* No. 4, April 1969, attributes to the woman the responsibility for introducing the child to the world of the irrational, of spirits, etc.
5. The term "universe" is used here in the sense P. L. Berger and T. Luckman use it in *The Social Construction of Reality* (New York: Doubleday and Co., Anchor Books, 1967).
6. Max Weber, *The Theory of Social and Economic Organization* (New York: MacMillan and Co., Free Press, 1964), p. 136.
7. *Ibid.,* p. 132.
8. More specifically, it condemned the practice of wearing wigs which seems to have been quite common among Arab women in the seventh century. [al-Bukhari, *Al-Jami as-Sahih,* p. 447 K: 67]. Tatooing, also condemned by Islam, is still practiced in Morocco, and some of the tatoos have unequivocal erotic meanings. [J. Herber, "Tatouage du Pubis Au Maroc," *Revue d'Ethne,* Vol. 3, 1922.]
9. Quran, Surah 24.
10. Abu Hamid al-Ghazali, *Revivification of Religious Sciences,* (Cairo: al-Maktaba at-Tijariya al-Kubra, n.d.), p. 35.
11. *Ibid.,* p. 28.
12. My data suggests that elderly women are actively seductive and apparently much more so than younger ones. Out of 402 letters, 13 report cases of men who have been seduced (according to their accounts) by mothers before noticing the daughter and wanting to marry her later. In many of these letters, men describe themselves, or are described, as having had a passive role in the process.
13. Malika Belghiti, "Les Relations Feminines Et Le Statut De La Femme Dans la Famille Rurale," *Collection du Bulletin Economique Et Social du Maroc* (Rabat: 1970), p. 57.
14. The French anthropologist Germaine Tillon in *Le Harem et les cousins,* (Paris: Editions du Souil, 1966) noticed that the peasant women, newly arrived to towns, usually adopt the practice of veiling. She found it strange that women who were not veiled before adopted veiling willingly. I think that this phenomenon could be very easily interpreted if one

remembers that for the rural woman who has recently emigrated to the town, the veil is a sign of upward mobility — the expression of her newly-acquired status as urbanite.

15. M. Belghiti, ''les Relations Femmenines,'' p. 58.
16. Women are especially restricted while in a space they should have a right to: the Mosque. In Morocco they may only use a specified area, usually a narrow, marginal, dark corner behind the male space. Although the Prophet allowed women to go to Mosques, their right to be there was, during Islam's fourteen centuries of existence, frequently in doubt and is still often subject to the husband's authorization. (al-Bukhari, *al-Jami' as-Sahih* p. 453. K: 67 B: 115.)
17. P. Pascon and M. Bentahar, ''Le Que Disent 269 Jeunes Ruraux,'' BESM, Jan-June 1965 XXXI, no. 112-113, p. 63.
18. E. Hall, *The Hidden Dimension* p. 156.
19. *Ibid.*, p. 163.
20. Erving Goffman, *Behavior in Public Places* (New York: MacMillan and Co., Free Press, 1966) p. 143.
21. Frantz Fanon, *A Dying Colonialism* (New York: Grove Press, Inc., 1967) p. 53. It is interesting to note that Fanon thought the incidents were ''funny.'' For a man with Fanon's sensitivity to segregation and preoccupation with revolutionary assertion of human rights, his remark is puzzling to say the least.
22. Personal communication by the Middle-Eastern observer.

NOTES TO CHAPTER 9

1. On the situation of the labor market, see A. Agouram and A. Belal, ''Bilab de l'Economie Marocaine Depuis l'Independence,'' *BESM,* XXXII, p. 116. According to the authors, unemployment in urban centers reaches 30% to 50% and hits 60% in rural areas. They emphasize the impact of this situation on the future by showing that while the number of laborers increases each year at a rate of 3%, the number of jobs increases at a rate of only 2%.
2. Emile Durkheim, ''L'Education Morale'' in *Selected Writings* edited by G. Giddins (Cambridge: Cambridge University Press, 1972) p. 174.
3. Mao-Tse-Tung, in Bruce Shaw's abridged version of Peking's authorized edition of *Selected Works of Mao-Tse-Tung* (New York: Harper and Row, 1970).
4. A decision to abolish pre-existing privileges, mainly those based on sexual differences, is a very daring decision on the part of any regime and more so on the part of a new regime. It is a very unpopular step indeed. The Chinese Communist Regime had to face and deal with the resistance the male Chinese population posed to such measures, see C. K. Yang, Chinese Communist Society: The Family and the Village (Cambridge, Mass.: M.I.T. Press, 1965) particulary Part I, ''The Chinese Family in the Communist Revolution.''
5. *1950 Marriage Law of the People's Republic of China,* Article 9.
6. Article 35, November 5, *Code du Statut Personnel.*
7. Personal communication from cadis and lawyers, supplemented by observation in Rabatis Sadad court during Februrary 1974.
8. A brief sketch of the history of the educational systems promoted by the French Protectorate in Morocco is in John Halstead's *Rebirth of a Nation: The Origin and Rise of Moroccan Nationalism 1912-1944* (Cambridge: Harvard University Press, Harvard Middle Eastern Monographs, 1969) pp. 98-114.
9. Fatema Hassar, ''The Special Problems of Young Women and Mothers with Regard to Their Families and Professional Careers,'' Read at the International Conference of Parents Associations, 22-28 July, 1962. Published by the Ministry of Education, Rabat. p. 85.
10. Allah Al Fasi, *The Independence Movements in Arab North Africa,* (New York: Octagon Books, 1970) p. 413.
11. Fatema Hassar, ''Special Problems of Young Women,'' p. 86.

12. *Le Maroc En Chiffres*, 2nd ed., (Rabat: Division des Statistiques et Banque Marocaine du Commerce Exterieur, 1971) p. 25.

13. Muhammed Lahbabi, *Les Annees 80 de Notre Jeunesse* (Casablanca: Editions Maghrebines, 1970) p. 55.

14. *Le Maroc en Chiffres*, p. 25.

15. All data in this section is taken from volume II of the *Recensement Generale de la Population et de la Habitat* (Royaume du Maroc: Secretariat d'Etat au Plan et au Developpement Regional, Direction de la Statistique, 1971) unless otherwise noted.

16. "Report on the Present Situation of the Moroccan Woman," Author anonymous. Read at the Second Afro-Asian Women's Conference at Ulan Bator, Mongolia in August of 1972. Published by the Permanent Secretariat of the Afro-Asian People's Solidarity Organization, Cairo.

17. *Ibid.*

18 *Recensement Generale de la Population*, 1971, vol. 2, p. 6.

19. *Ibid.*, p. 12.

20. *Ibid.*, p. 6.

21. Wilhelm Reich, *The Mass Psychology of Fascism* (New York: Farrar, Strauss and Giroux, 1970) p. 60.

22. *Ibid.*, p. 31.

23. *Ibid.*, p. 55.

24. See *Honor and Shame, The Values of Mediterranean Society*, edited by J. G. Peristiany (Chicago: The University of Chicago Press, 1966). Peristiany's introduction is a concise description of the psycho-social mechanisms operating under the concept of honor. One feature of these mechanisms is that the men in such societies do not have a source of self-esteem within themselves but only attached to subjects outside themselves.

25. J. Whiting and I. Child, *Child Training and Personality*, (New Haven: Yale University Press, 1953) p. 276.

26. W. Reich, *Mass Psycholgy of Fascism*, p. 32.

NOTES TO CONCLUSION

1. Mariarosa Della Costa, *Women and the Subversion of the Community*. Bristol, England: Falling Wall Press, Ltd., 1972.

2. On the specific question of child care, See *Women and Child Care in China* by Ruth Sidel, Baltimore, Maryland: Penguin Books, Inc., 1973. On the condition of women in general, see *Fashen* by William Hinton, New York: Vintage Books, 1966; and *Chinese Communist Society, the Family and the Village*, by C. K. Yang, Cambridge, Mass.; MIT Press.

3. "Communism in Marriage," article by David Raizanov, published in Moscow in 1926, reproduced in *Al-Mar,a Wa al-Ishtiraguya* (The Women and Socialism), translated and edited by George Tarabishi, Beirut: Dar al-Abad, 1974 (second edition), pp. 33 thru 70.

4. Dr. Salwa Hamachi, *Al-Mar'a al-Alabiya Wa-lmuj Tama' at-Paqlidiy* (The Arab Woman and the Underdeveloped Traditional Society), Beirut: Maktabat Al-Alam At-Talit, Dar Al Aquiqua, 1973, particularly Chapter V (the relation between the sexes) and Chapter VII (the position of the wife).

5. George Tarabishi, in his introduction to *Al-Mar'a Wa al-Ishtiraquiya*, p. 13.

6. Moroccan Penal Code, Article 418: "Le meurtre, les blessures et les coups sont excusables s'ils sont commis par l'epoux sur son epouse ainsi que sur le complice a l'instant ou il les surprend en flagrant d'elit d'adultre."

7. Philip Slater, *The Glory of Hera*, p. 73.

8. Al-Majdoub, p. 144

9. Dr. Jalal Sadek al'Adm, *Fi Lhubbi Wa Lhubbi Al Udri* (On Love and Udrite Love), second edition, Beirut: Dar al-Aouda, 1974, p. 92 and following.

10. Dr. Jalal al'Adm, *Fi Lhubbi*.

11. Tahar Labib Djedidi, "La Poesie Amoureuse des Arabes," Algeirs: SNED, Etudes et Documents, 1974.

12. *Ibid.*, 76, 134, 140, 142.

13. Dr. Jalal Sadek al'Adm, *Fi Lhubbi*, pp. 110-111.

14. *Ibid.*, p. 28.

15. Abdallah Laroui, "La Crise des Intellectuels Arabes," paper read at colloquium in Louvain, 1970, published in *La Crise des Intellectuels Arabes*, Paris: Maspero, 1974.

16. George Tarabishi, introduction to *Al Mar'a Wa al-Ishtiraquiya*, p. 13.

GLOSSARY

Aisha Kandisha	a female demon who takes possession of people
'amlu triq	make way!
aruba	a beautiful woman in love with her husband
aryana	nude, unveiled
'azl	coitus interruptus
ba'al	lord and owner, patrilineal marriage
baghaya	prostitute
Code	Code du Statut Personnel, the laws relating to the individual and the family
fitna	chaos, an irresistibly beautiful woman
guellassa	cashier of a *hammam*
hajr	a man's refusal to communicate with his wife or concubine
hammam	turkish bath
hiba	the act by which a woman offered herself to a man
Hijra	622 AD, the year one of the Muslim calendar, the beginning of civilization
hma	mother-in-law
	descendants of Ali
htewta	little penis (in Moroccan Arabic)
idda	period a woman must wait after being divorced or widowed before she can remarry
ila	a woman's right to divorce her husband if he swears an oath not to have sexual intercourse with her for four months and he keeps his oath
Jahiliya	before 622 AD, the time of barbarism and ignorance
karh	hateful, a new wife's refusal to communicate with her husband
khul'	a woman's right to buy her freedom from her husband

lalla	my mistress
ma'	waterdrop, sperm or ova
muhsan	a married person, thus one who should be protected against the sin of unlawful intercourse
mut'a	pleasure, temporary marriage
qaid	cunning
sadica	female friend, matrilineal marriage
Sharia	the divine law
shia	Muslims who believe in the authority of descendants of Ali
sidi	master
sira	biography of the Prophet
sunna	the right path, the orthodox way
surah	a chapter of the Quran
tamlik	the husband's delegation of his authority to his wife
teyyaba	girl friday of a *hammam*
Umma	the community of believers in Islam
zina	illicit intercourse

BIBLIOGRAPHY

ABBOTT, Nabia. *Aichah, the Beloved of Mohammed*. Chicago: The University of Chicago Press, 1942.

ABBOTT, B. "Women and the State in Early Islam." *Journal of Near Eastern Studies*, Vol. I, Jan.-Oct., 1942.

ACHOUR, M. "Vue particuliere du problems de l'environement en fonction du milieu scolaire marocain." Rabat: *Maroc-Medical*, December 1964.

AMIN, Kacem. *Tahrir al-Mar'a*. Cairo: Umum al-Makatib Bimisr Walharij, 1928.

AMIN, Samir. *Le Maghreb Modern*. Paris: Les Editions de Minuit, 1970

al-AQQAD, Abbas Mahmud. *al-Mar'a Fil-Qur'an*. Cairo: Dar al-Hilal, n.d.

BARRY, H. III, CHILD, I., BACON, M. "A Cross-Cultural Survey of Some Sex Differences in Socialization." *Journal of Abnormal and Social Psychology*, Vol. 55, November 1957.

BEETSON, A. F. L. "The So-Called Harlots of Hadramaout." *Oriens* V, 1952.

BELGHITI, Malika. *Les Relations Femmenines et le Statut de la Femme dans la Famille Rurale*. Rabat: Collection du Bulletin Economique et Social du Maroc, 1970.

BLOCHET, E. *Le culte d'Aphrodite: Anahita chez les Arabs du Paganisme*. Chalon-s-Saone, 1902.

BONNET, C. "Reflexions sur l'influence du milieu familial traditionnel sur la structuration de la personnalite au Maroc." *Revue de Neuropsychiatrie Infantile*, Vol. 18, No. 10-11.

BOUSQUET, G. H. *Ethique Sexuelle de l'Islam*. Paris: G. P. Maisonneuve et Larose, 1966.

al-BUKHARI, Abu Abd Allah Muhammad Ibn Ismail. *Kitab al-Jami' as-Sahih*. Leyden, Holland: Ludolf Krehl, 1868.

COSER, Rose L. *The Family, its Structure and Functions*. New York: St. Martin's Press, 1964.

ELLIS, Havelock. *On Life and Sex (Essays on Love and Virtue)*. New York: New American Library, Mentor Books, 1957.

ENGELS, F. *The Origin of the Family, Private Property and the State*. New York: Pulerwalund Publishers, 1970.

"Enquete d'opinion sur la planification familiale." Part I in *Milieu Urbain*, Part II in *Milieu Rural*. Royaume du Maroc: Ministere de la Sante-Publique, Secretariat d'Etat au Plan, Division des Statistiques, 1966.

FARES, Edouard. *L'Honneur Chez les Arabes Avant l'Islam, Etude de Sociologie*. Paris: Librairie d'Amerique et d'Orient, 1932.

al-FASI, Allal. *The Independence Movements in Arab North-Africa*. New York: Octagon Books, 1970.

FENICHEL, Otto. *The Psychoanalytic Theory of Neurosis*. New York: Norton and Co. 1945.

FERENCZI, Sandor. *Thalassa: A Theory of Genitality*. New York: Norton and Co. 1968.

FIRESTONE, Shulamith. *The Dialectic of Sex.* New York: Bantam Books, 1970.

FORGET, Nelly. "Attitude a l'egard du travail professionel de la femme du Maroc." *Image de la femme dans la Societe.* Paul-Henry Chambart de Lauwe, ed. Paris: Les Editions Ovrieres, 1964.

FREUD, Sigmund. *A General Introduction to Psycho-analysis.* New York: Pocket Books, 1952.

FREUD, Sigmund. *New Introductory Lectures on Psychoanalysis.* New York: Norton and Co., 1965.

FREUD, Sigmund. *The Ego and the Id.* New York: Norton and Co., 1962

FREUD, Sigmund. *The Future of an Illusion.* New York: Doubleday and Co., Anchor Books, 1964.

FREUD, Sigmund. *Civilization and its Discontents.* New York: Norton and Co., 1962.

FREUD, Sigmund. *Sexuality and the Psychology of Love.* New York: Collier Books, 1963.

FREUD, Sigmund. *Three Contributions to the Theory of Sex.* New York: E. P. Dutton and Co., Second Edition, 1909.

FREUD, Sigmund. *The Sexual Enlightenment of Children.* New York: Collier Books, 1963.

FREUD, Sigmund. *Group Psychology and the Analysis of the Ego.* New York: Bantam Books, 1970.

FORD, Clellan S. and BEACH, Frank A. *Patterns of Sexual Behavior.* New York: Harper and Row, 1970.

FOX, Robin. *Kinship and Marriage.* New York: Penguin Books, Pelican Books, 1967.

GAUDRY, Mathea. *Le femme chaouia de l'Aures etude de sociologie Berbere.* Librairie Orientaliste Paul Geuthuer, 1929.

al-GHAZALI, Abu-Hamid. *Ihya Ulum ad-Din.* Cairo: al-Maktaba at-Tijariya al-Kubra, n.d.

al-GHAZALI, Abu-Hamid. *Mizan al-'Amal.* Cairo: Dar al-Ma'arif, 1964.

GOETHALS, George W. "Factors Affecting Permissive and Non-Permissive Rules Regarding Premarital Sex." *The Sociology of Sex: A Book of Readings.* James H. Heuselin, ed. New York: Appleton-Century-Croft, 1971.

GOFFMAN, Erving. *Behavior in Public Places.* New York: MacMillan and Co., Free Press, 1966.

GOFFMAN, Erving. *The Presentation of Self in Everyday Life.* New York: Doubleday and Co., Anchor Books, 1959.

GOFFMAN, Erving. *Encounters.* New York: Bobbs-Merrill Co., 1961.

GOFFMAN, Erving. *Strategic Interaction.* New York: Random House, Ballantine Books, 1969.

al-HAJOUI, Mohammad. *al-Mar'a Bayna as-Shar' wal-Qanun.* Casablanca: Matabi' Dar al-Kitab, n.d.

HALL, Edward T. *The Hidden Dimension.* New York: Doubleday and Co., Anchor Books, 1969.

HALL, Edward T. *The Silent Language*. New York: Fawcett World Library, Premier Books, 1969.

HINTON, W. *Fanshen, A Documentary of Revolution in a Chinese Village*. New York: Vintage Books, Random House, 1968.

HORNEY, Karen. *"Feminine Psychology*. New York: Norton and Co., 1973.

HORNEY, Karen. "The Flight for Womanhood: The Masculinity Complex in Woman, as Viewed by Men and Women." *International Journal of Psychoanalysis*. Vol. 7, 1926.

IBN HISHAM, ed. *Sirat an-Nabi*. Written by Ibn Ishaq. Cairo: Matba'at al-Madani, 1963.

IBN KHALDUN. *The Muqaddimah, An Introduction to History*. (translated from the Arabic by Franz Rosenthal) Princeton, N.J.: Bollinger Series, Princeton University Press, 1969.

IBN SAAD. *Kitab at-Tabaqat al-Kubra*. Beirut: Dar Beyrouth, 1958.

al-ISBAHANI, Abu-al-Faraj. *Kitab al-Aghani*. Cairo: Matba'at at-Taqaddum, n.d. (Except for Volume 16, which is from *Kitab al-Aghani*. Beirut: Dar at-Taqafa, 1909.)

JUNG, C. G. *Psychology and Religion*. New Haven: Yale University Press, 1969.

KARDINER, Abraham. *Sex and Morality*. New York: Bobbs-Merrill Co., 1962.

KINSEY, Alfred C., MARTIN, Clyde E., GEBHARD, Paul H., and POMEROY, Wardell B. *Sexual Behavior in the Human Female*. New York: Pocket Book Edition, 1965.

KINSEY, Alfred C., POMEROY, W. G. and MARTIN, Clyde E. *Sexual Behavior in the Human Male*. Philadelphia: W. B. Saunders, 1948.

LAING, R. D., and ESTERSON. *Sanity, Madness and the Family*. Baltimore: Penguin Books, Pelican Books, 1964.

LAROUI, Abdallah. *L'ideologie Arabe Contemporaine*. Paris: Francois Maspero, 1967.

LAROUI, Abdallah. *L'Histoire du Maghreb, Un Essai de Synthese*. Paris: Francois Maspero, 1970.

LENIN. *On the Emancipation of Women*. Moscow: Progress Publishers, n.d.

LEVY, Reuben. *The Social Structure of Islam*. London: Cambridge University Press, 1957.

MALIK, Ibn Anas. *al-Muwatta*. Cairo: Mustafa al-Babi al-Halabi, n.d.

MALINOWSKI, Bronislaw. *The Sexual Life of Savages*. New York: Harcourt, Brace and World, 1929.

MALINOWSKI, Bronislaw. *Sex and Repression in Savage Society*. New York: Farrar, Strauss & Giroux, Noonday Press, 1955.

MAO TSE-TUNG. *Selected Works of Mao-Tse-Tung*, from the authorized Peking Edition. New York: Harper and Row, 1970.

MARCUSE, Herbert. *Eros and Civilization*. New York: Random House, Vintage Books, 1955.

MARTENSON, M. "Attituds vis-a-vis du travail professionnel de la femme maroccaine." *Bulletin Economique et Social du Maroc*, XXVIII, Jan.-March 1966.

MARX, Karl. *Pre-Capitalist Economic Formations*. New York: International Publishers, 1965.

MARX, Karl. *On Colonialism and Modernization*. New York: Doubleday and Co., Anchor Books, 1969.

MARX, Karl. *Capital*. New York: International Publishers, 1967.

MEAD, Margaret. *Male and Female: A Study of the Sexes in a Changing World*. New York: Dell Publishing Co., 1968.

MILL, John Stuart. *On the Subjection of Women*. Fawcett New York: World Library, Premier Books, 1971.

MILLETT, Kate. *Sexual Politics*. New York: Avon Books, 1971.

MITSCHERLICH, Alexander. *Society Without the Father*. New York: Schocken Books, 1970.

M'RABET, Fadelo. *Les Algeriennes*. Paris: Francois Maspero, 1967.

AL-MUNAJID, Salah ad-Din. *al-Hayat al-Jinsiya, Indah al-Arab*. Beirut: Dar al-Kitab al-Jadid, 1958.

MUSA, Salama. *al-Mar'a Laysat Lu'batu ar-Rajul*. Cairo: Salama Musa Li-nashr wa Tawzi', 1955.

MUSLIM, Abu-al-Hasan. *al-Jami' as-Sahih*. Beirut: al-Maktab at-Tijari, n.d.

NEWMANN, Erich. *The Great Mother: An Analysis of the Archetype*. Princeton, N.J.: Princeton University Press, Bollinger Series, 1972.

NOUACEUR, Khadija. "Evolution du travail professionnel de la femme au Maroc." *Image de la Femme dans la Societe*. Ed. Paul-Henry Chambart de Lauwe. Paris: Les Editions Ouvrieres, 1964.

OPLER, Marvin K. "Woman's Social Status and the Forms of Marriage." *American Journal of Sociology*, Vol. 49, 1943-1944.

PARSONS, Talcott. *Social Structure and Personality*. New York: MacMillan and Co., Free Press, 1970.

PASCON, P., AND BENTAHAR, M. "Ce que disent 269 jeunes ruraux." *Bulletin Economique et Social du Maroc*, XXXI, No. 112-113, Jan.-June 1969.

PATAI, R. *Sex and the Family in the Bible and the Middle East*. New York: Doubleday and Co., 1959.

PERISTIANY, J. G., ed. *Honor and Shame, the Values of Mediterranean Society*. Chicago: The University of Chicago Press, 1966.

PESLE, O. *La femme Musulmane Dans le Droit, la Religion et les Maurs*. Rabat: Editions Laporte, 1946.

PICKTHALL, Mohammad Marmaduke. *The Meaning of the Glorious Koran*. New York: New American Library, Mentor Books, thirteenth printing, n.d.

RADCLIFFE-BROWN, A. R. *Structure and Function in Primitive Society*. New York: MacMillan and Co., Free Press, 1965.

RADCLIFFE-BROWN, A. R. and FORDE, Daryll, eds. *African Systems of Kinship and Marriage*. London: Oxford University Press, 1950.

RADI, Abdelwahad. "Processus de socialization de l'enfant Moroccain." *Etudes Philosophiques et Litteraires.* No. 4, April 1969.

REICH, WILHELM. *The Mass Psychology of Fascism.* New York: Farrar, Strauss and Giroux, 1970.

REICH, Wilhelm. *The Sexual Revolution.* New York: Farrar, Strauss and Giroux, 1970.

REIK, Theodor. *Of Love and Lust: On the Psychoanalysis of Romantic and Sexual Emotions.* New York: Bantam Books, 1957.

ROLAND, D. J. L. "Developpement de le personnalite et Incidences de l'Environnement au Maroc." Rabat: *Maroc Medical,* Dec. 1964.

RUITENBEEK, Hendrick M., ed. *Sexuality and Identity.* New York: Dell Publishing Co., 1970.

RUITENBEEK, Hendrik M., ed. *Psychoanalysis and Female Sexuality.* New Haven, Conn.: College and University Press, 1966.

RYCKMANS, C. *Les Religions Arabes Preislamiques.* Louvain: Institut Orientaliste Louvain, 1951.

SCHACHT, Joseph. *An Introduction to Islamic Law.* London: Oxford University Press, 1964.

SLATER, Philip. *The Glory of Hera: Greek Mythology and the Greek Family.* Boston: Beacon Press, 1968.

SLATER, Philip E. and SLATER, Doris. "Maternal Ambivalence and Narcissism: A Cross-Cultural Study." *Merrill-Palmer Quarterly of Behavior and Development,* Vol. II, No. 8, 1965.

SMITH, W. Robertson. *Kinship and Marriage in Early Arabia.* Boston: Beacon Press, 1903.

STERN, Gertrude H. *Marriage in Early Islam.* London: The Royal Asiatic Society, 1939.

AT-TARMIDI, Abu 'Issa. *Sunan at-Tarmidi.* Medina: al-Maktaba as-Salafiya, n.d.

THOMPSON, Clara M. *On Women.* New York: New American Library, Mentor Books, 1971.

TILLON, Germaine. *Le Harem et les Cousins.* Paris: Editions Du Seuil, 1966.

VEBLEN, Thorstein. *The Theory of the Leisure Class.* New York: New American Library, Mentor Books, 1953.

WATT, W. Montgomery. *Muhammad at Mecca.* London: Oxford University Press, 1953.

WATT, W. Montgomery. *Muhammad at Medina.* London: Oxford University Press, 1956.

WATT, W. Montgomery. *Muhammad Prophet and Statesman.* London: Oxford University Press, 1961.

WEBER, Max. *Economy and Religion.* New York: Bedminster Press, 1968.

WESTERMARCK, Edward. *Wit and Wisdom in Morocco: A Study of Native Proverbs.* London: George Routledge and Sons, 1930.

WESTERMARCK, Edward. *Ritual and Belief in Morocco.* London: MacMillan and Co., 1926.

doesn't have   Wedding Ceremonies.

WHITING, Beatrice. "Sex Identity Conflict and Physical Violence: A Comparative Study." *American Anthropoligist.* Vol. 67, No. 6, Part 2, Dec. 1965.

WHITING, John, and BURTON, R. "The Absent Father and Cross-Sex Identity," *Merrill-Palmer Quarterly of Behavior and Development,* Vol. 7, No. 2, 1961.

WHITING, John and CHILD, Irwin. *Child Training and Personality: A Cross-Cultural Study.* New Haven, Conn.: Yale University Press, 1971.

YANG, C. K. *Chinese Communist Society: The Family and The Village.* Cambridge, Mass.: M.I.T. Press, 1965.